M000017166

ENDORSEMENTS

Einstein said, "If the answer is simple, God is speaking." The Bible is undoubtedly incredibly complex, yet in the hands of a gifted teacher it is not complicated. The best teachers don't tell you what to think but help you learn how to think, or as this title implies, how to see clearly. Steve is one of the most gifted Bible teachers of our day. His ability to take the complex and make it accessible to the masses with beautiful simplicity is both inviting and empowering.

For nearly a decade Steve's understanding of Scripture has profoundly impacted my walk with God and my ministry. *Seeing Through a Better Lens* condenses the best of a lifetime of learning into a book that brings incredible clarity to the often complicated and sparks a lifetime love affair with the Bible. I'm excited and grateful that the perspective contained in Steve's head and heart are now offered to the world in this book!

— Joel Lowry,
Lead Pastor of Sozo Church

Seeing Through A Better Lens provides a refreshing and much needed understanding of how good the Good News really is. It is full of rich, biblical insight as well as glimpses into Steve's own personal journey of encountering the glory of the New Covenant. It is my joy to recommend both the book and its author. Enjoy!

— Chuck Maher,
Associate Leader at Kingdom Life San Antonio,
Founder of Maher Ministries

In his book, Seeing Through a Better Lens, Steve Smothers does a masterful job of teaching, inspiring, challenging, confronting, and most of all encouraging his readers to live our life in Christ the way Jesus intended for us to live. We are urged to remain focused on Jesus, understanding that He is the main theme of the Bible. Steve's insights into God's Kingdom are nothing short of revelation that will help every reader pursue everything God has in this life with laser focus. In addition, Steve unfolds the book of Hebrews in a way that makes it come alive.

I highly recommend this book to anyone! It doesn't matter if you've been a student of the Bible for many years or if you're just beginning, you will benefit from *Seeing Through a Better Lens*.

— **Charles Patterson,**
Charles Patterson Ministries

Thank you, Steve, for a thought-provoking book. It's laid out in a way that is really easy to read. I like the short paragraphs and bullet points. They make it possible to quickly get the big picture and then dive in later for deeper study.

For people with little or no theological training, this offers a great introduction that will put the reader on a good theological path. For people with a lot of theological baggage, this is definitely a thought-provoking book! I would advise reading it through and allowing yourself to be provoked.

— **Tommie Naumann,**
Missionary, DMM Leader, Thessaloniki, Greece

Steve is a wonderful teacher. This clearly comes across both in his preaching and in this book. What I find so refreshing is that Steve is able to take profound truths and put them across in plain English—his is a gift for making the complex readily understandable. Often humorous and always insightful, his teachings lead to the powerful outcome of deepening your walk with God. He takes essential truths and conveys them in such a way that you really get it, and it changes your way of thinking. His understanding of the teachings of Scripture is profound, and your understanding will become more profound as you engage with this material. I wholeheartedly recommend this book for people who are young in the faith and to those who have walked the Christian path for many years.

— The Rev. Hugh Bromiley,
Director Beth Shalom Inner Healing Ministries

I have witnessed the Gospel with more clarity, catching its infectious liberation and unbridled joy, through sharing life's journey with Steve Smothers—my pastor, mentor, spiritual father, and friend for over thirty years. Steve has brought to light many of the same inspirational and soul-altering truths in his newest book, *Seeing Through A Better Lens.* I invite you to walk with him through these pages, so you, too, can be captivated afresh by the stunning beauty of God's grace toward you.

— Jason Lohse,
Author, Pastor, Worship Leader

Decades of studying and experience are condensed to create a book of great depth yet comprehensible to the non-biblical scholar. Steve has a gift for breaking down complex ideas and historical accounts to help the reader receive greater insight into the Bible and its covenants. Without an understanding of the covenants, we will miss the significance of the relationship between God and humanity. Once we understand God's deep loving relationship with us and His progressive revelation of Himself in the Scripture, we can begin to thrive in our identity and relationship with God and others.

Steve's anointing in teaching has helped me understand these concepts that will forever change my relationship with God and everyone around me. We are truly living under a Better Covenant.

— LaTisha McIntyre,
School Teacher & Missionary

Steve Smothers is one of the most effective disciple-makers I've known in the USA. From my first encounter with Steve, it was clear to me that he was a work in progress—a learner in progress. A disciple is literally a "learner"! Steve really "gets it" and understood early in his ministry that making disciples is more important than anything else, except for being a disciple.

From the beginning, Steve has been all about leadership development through making disciples. It's only natural for him to write about what he's been learning and teaching. Steve knows what he's talking about and talks about it well, because he lives it.

Steve possesses the rare mix of a substantial knowledge of the Scriptures, a wise sense of how life works best, and a stubborn focus on the person of Jesus. In fact, this book is another arrow in the quiver of the "Jesus way of thinking," as opposed to our "old religious way of thinking." Steve has an in-your-face approach with a compassionate, persuasive touch —which is a breath of fresh air for those who are still clinging to their "Churchianity."

In a world of super-spirituality, celebrity gurus, constant promotion of the Sunday show, and the annoying shallowness all around us, Steve Smothers is the real deal. This new book makes the reality of BETTER COVENANT discipleship available for all. Every time I'm with Steve, I hear something new for me to apply. In essence, our meetings always result in us sharpening one another. And the best thing for me is that I can count Steve Smothers as a good brother and a faithful friend!

— Tim Timmons,
Speaker, Author of *Simply Enough! Jesus Plus Nothing*

The amount of Christian writers who have written about Christ is enormous, but the brave few who have written of our union with Christ is minuscule by comparison. Steve has tackled my favorite topic and what I consider to be the most mind melting verse of the Bible (John 14:20) with scholarly excellence. But the thing about this book that I find so refreshing is the manner in which the layout carves out bite sized morsels of Gospel wisdom and feed them to you in an order that is much like leaping from stone to stone in crossing a sea of wisdom. I found myself meditating on an italicized paragraph long after I had read it. It's an eternal word for the fast paced life that will make you slow down and take in the majesty of our reconciled union with God.

— Bill Vanderbush,
Speaker, Pastor, Author of *Reckless Grace*

Seeing Through A Better Lens
Copyright © 2019 Steve K. Smothers

Bracketed text within Scripture quotations is the author's emphasis.

All Scripture quotations, unless otherwise indicated, are taken from the Holy Bible, New International Version®, NIV®. Copyright ©1973, 1978, 1984, 2011 by Biblica, Inc.™ Used by permission of Zondervan. All rights reserved worldwide. www.zondervan.comThe "NIV" and "New International Version" are trademarks registered in the United States Patent and Trademark Office by Biblica, Inc.™

Other scripture quotations are from:

Scripture quotations marked TPT are from The Passion Translation®. Copyright © 2017, 2018 by Passion & Fire Ministries, Inc. Used by permission. All rights reserved. ThePassionTranslation.com.

Scripture quotations marked (ESV) are from The ESV® Bible (The Holy Bible, English Standard Version®), copyright © 2001 by Crossway, a publishing ministry of Good News Publishers. Used by permission. All rights reserved.

Scripture quotations taken from the New American Standard Bible® (NASB), Copyright © 1960, 1962, 1963, 1968, 1971, 1972, 1973, 1975, 1977, 1995 by The Lockman Foundation Used by permission. www.Lockman.org

ISBN: 978-1-7330596-0-2 (*paperback*)
ISBN: 978-1-7330596-1-9 (*ebook*)

Cover and interior design by Ryan Smothers

Edited by Karen Steinmann

Printed in the United States of America

Published by Steve K. Smothers
Austin, Texas, USA
Visit SteveKSmothers.com

SEEING THROUGH A
BETTER LENS

We've all been handed a lens that determines how we read the Bible and perceive God, ourselves, and others. A Better Covenant lens opens our imaginations to see just how vast and inclusive God's Kingdom really is.

STEVE K. SMOTHERS
**Foreword by JACK R. TAYLOR
and ROBERT R. MEARNS**

CONTENTS

DEDICATION x

ACKNOWLEDGMENTS xi

FOREWORD
By Jack R. Taylor xii
By Robert R. Mearns xiii

INTRODUCTION 1

CHAPTER ONE
REPENTANCE IS A GOOD WORD 7
Aligning With God's Way of Thinking

CHAPTER TWO
THE JESUS LENS 23
Seeing the Bible Through A Better Lens

CHAPTER THREE
THE GOODNESS OF GOD 43
Understanding the Father Heart of God

CHAPTER FOUR
A STORY OF COVENANT AND KINGDOM 69
With Whom are You Agreeing?

CHAPTER FIVE
LIVING FROM THE RIGHT SIDE OF THE CROSS 99
Better Covenant Discipleship

CHAPTER SIX
STORIES OF THE ADVANCING KINGDOM 119
What's Your 'Kingdom of Heaven is Like' Story?

APPENDIX
Why Use the Language of Better Covenant 147
Instead of New Covenant?

NOTES 159

DEDICATION

I dedicate this book to my Sozo Church family and especially to my friend and lead pastor, Joel Lowry, who helped develop and cultivate many of the book's ideas. Much of the material here was field tested at Sozo Life in spring 2018. Sozo Church, your encouragement was this book's impetus, and I am so grateful.

I dedicate this book to my family, who has walked with me every step of the way on this journey of BETTER COVENANT living. Lesa, you have always been my biggest cheerleader and best friend. Your love, support, and prayer have made this book a reality. Ryan, thanks for believing in your dad and giving so much of your time to help with formatting and creative suggestions. Josh and Beth, most of this book was written just before your wedding; thanks for your understanding and support! Caleb and Ali, your zest for adventure inspires me, and your cookies do, too. Nathan and Judah, you guys are my favorite worship leaders! You host His presence well.

I am truly a blessed man to be surrounded by such an encouraging tribe of friends and family! Your passion to pursue the KINGDOM OF GOD and BETTER COVENANT living is an inspiration for me to keep writing, equipping, and being Papa Steve to those who long for Kingdom-family.

ACKNOWLEDGMENTS

Nothing in life is successful without the combined effort of many gifted people who are willing to contribute their time, talent, and passion for a common goal. I gratefully give thanks to:

- Ryan Smothers for his hours of formatting, technical assistance, and unending encouragement.

- Karen Steinmann and LaTisha McIntyre for your editing and proofreading skills.

- Jason Lohse for encouraging me to write this book, and for helping me navigate my way through the process.

A FOREWORD BY JACK R. TAYLOR

In my adventure with books, my first consideration is that of knowing the author! One does not have to be long with Steve Smothers to realize that he has a heart for making disciples for Jesus Christ! Reading the Table of Contents reveals much about this book's heart and direction. The reader of this volume is very likely to be quickly led into an adventure of life-altering revelation.

Any presentation that proves effective will start at the right place and proceed in sequences toward an ordered conclusion. I love the obvious path this volume takes, from repentance to advancing the KINGDOM.

Among the strongest emphases, the reader will find the book to be KINGDOM to the core. This is all to say that this stands as no ordinary book but, indeed, offers a challenge to claim the blessings of Kingdom-understanding, Kingdom-engagement, Kingdom-encounters, and Kingdom-demonstrations.

Thanks, Steve, for creating a masterpiece!

Jack Taylor, President
Dimensions Ministries
Melbourne, Florida

A FOREWORD BY ROBERT R. MEARNS

Through the decades I have known Steve, he has been motivated with a passion for discipling one-on-one. Steve Smothers has lived his message by facilitating others, even if it means early morning breakfasts or late nights on the back porch. He has always made time for others. As a disciple or follower of Jesus, Steve serves others—an uncommon example in an age obsessed with leadership's power, position, and prestige.

Steve challenges our paradigms of thinking, or should I say "seeing." This book awakens a longing to keep learning and not just settle for our preferred traditions, defending them against other views. We only grow old when we stop learning.

Steve shares insights with clear contextual and situational information, which helped me better grasp the distinct transition from the Old Covenant to the New Covenant. Blurred vision causes hesitation and inaction. The challenge is to move forward into our inheritance—to move from the shadow of typology to the experience of a relationship with the Abba of Jesus, who loves and accepts us unconditionally. This clean lens certainly shows The Way we were intended to live in communion with the Light of the World—and light does not have a shadow! Jesus taught His disciples by example to hear what Father was saying and see what Father was doing.

Jesus met a rich young ruler who had earnestly sought to keep the many laws. *The Passion Translation* reads, *"Jesus fixed his gaze upon the man, with tender love"* (Mark 10:21). He challenged him to leave what he was attached to (his wealth) and come follow Him. It radically changes our perspective when we see people through the compassionate lens of God's love . . . *"He loved him"* translates as *"with a fixed and sustained gaze filled with interest, love and concern."* Just a glancing look takes but a moment; seeing requires us to process information, connect dots, empathize, and understand. The result is a love expressed; otherwise, it is just an idea.

Seeing Through a Better Lens is a book I will return to again —next time with a highlighter in hand. Thank you, Steve, for encouraging me to live present and see a future designed for me as I seek to live this abundant life from Heaven's perspective with the veil removed—a much better lens!

Robert R. Mearns, President
Kingsway Connection
Granite Falls, North Carolina

INTRODUCTION

In November 2018, I felt prompted to write a book based on a message I had taught at Sozo Church the year before called "Living from the Right Side of the Cross." As I jotted down the initial topics I wanted to cover, I soon realized that I had enough information for several books. Shortly after, the idea of a series of books about BETTER COVENANT DISCIPLESHIP was born.

Though my heart was, and still is, to illustrate what living from the right side of the cross should look like, I now realize that establishing the proper foundation proves crucial. Therefore, the first book in this series is entitled *Seeing Through a Better Lens*.

FIND YOUR WHY

Simon Sinek's YouTube video, *Find Your Why*, helped me understand the reason I needed to start this series of books with *Seeing Through a Better Lens*. According to Sinek,

> "Those who inspire are separated from the rest because they start with '*the why*.' Being confident in your *why* is the only thing that will truly inspire others and sustain you in difficult times."[1]

Many years ago as a 20-year-old youth pastor in a traditional church, I found myself in trouble because I asked so many *why* questions. My curiosity was perceived as rebellion. I was seen as a troublemaker because I was questioning the way things had always been done. In truth, I simply wanted to understand the purpose behind what we were doing. I wanted to know the vision of my senior leaders. I wasn't trying to rock their boat; I was trying to secure mine. I wanted to be a better team player, not a rebel.

Getting *the why* right is central to the success of everything we do. Sinek believes,

> "It is our *why* that creates motivation to get out of bed and go to work. *Why* creates the culture at our place of work, home, church, etc. *Why* is the foundation we return to when we veer off course and wonder, 'Why am I even doing this?' We must have a compelling answer to why we do everything we do; otherwise, our ventures will become mundane and meaningless —no matter how 'successful' our metrics or others say we are."[2]

A lot of unfulfilled millionaires exist in the world because they've lost their *why*. They quietly wonder, "What's the point? There's got to be more!" And there is, but they won't find fulfillment in what they do, no matter how efficiently they do it, unless they have a large enough *why* that continually motivates them. Satisfaction comes from fulfilling your destiny and purpose in life. And truthfully, deep satisfaction is only found in fulfilling God's vision of advancing His KINGDOM through NEW COVENANT living!

Sinek's message of *Finding Your Why* is constructed around three concentric circles: The inner circle is the *why*. The next circle out from the center is the *how*. The outer circle is the *what*.

THE WHY

I believe Jesus' ministry on earth illustrates the principle of the *why*. Everything He initiated flowed from the purpose for which He came to earth. In His Sermon on the Mount (Matthew 5-7), Jesus shared His revolutionary dream of the KINGDOM OF GOD on earth as it is in heaven. He lived and imparted His why everywhere He went.

From the beginning of His ministry, Jesus inspired others with His vision and message of the KINGDOM OF GOD.

The time has come, the Kingdom of God has come near. Repent and believe the good news (Mark 1:15).

Jesus' why is simple but profound. The KINGDOM OF GOD is now in our midst. We must change our way of thinking and align with the mind of our true King. As we believe and embrace Jesus as Lord and King, our lives are transformed from the inside out. And this is truly GOOD NEWS!

Seeing Through a Better Lens, along with the upcoming books *Something New and Better* and *How to Make Sense of the Bible,* lays out God's vision of the NEW COVENANT and KINGDOM OF GOD.

THE WHAT

Living from the right side of the cross is what we should all desire as NEW COVENANT, KINGDOM disciples. This is the subject matter of the subsequent two books in this series, *Living from the Right Side of the Cross* and *Victory on the Right Side of the Cross.*

Here's a sample of some of the topics covered in these books:

- Worship: Experiencing God's Circle of Shared Life

- Identity: Restored and Empowered

- Separation or Union?

- Spiritual Warfare: It's All About Authority and Agreement

- Prayer: Forgiveness and the Language of the Holy Spirit

- The KINGDOM OF GOD: The Left-Handed Power of God

- Kingdom Communion: Life Since Jesus Killed Religion

- Holiness: Shifting My Worldview

- Spiritual Practices: Cultivating the Unforced Rhythms of Grace

- Stories of the Advancing Kingdom

- What About Physical Healing?

- What About Prophetic Ministry?

- Vocation: Incarnational Living

- Marriage and Family: Love Always Wins!

- Women: Back to the Garden, Forward in BETTER COVENANT LIVING

- Giving: From Tithing to BETTER COVENANT Generosity

- Leadership Culture: Fathering, Equipping, and Serving

- Eschatology: When Will the End of the Age Come?

- Evangelism: The Jesus Movement

- World Missions: Advancing the KINGDOM OF HEAVEN

- Plus **More!**

THE HOW

So, how do I do what I want to do? Jesus declared that the way one enters the KINGDOM OF GOD and His story of NEW COVENANT living is through repentance (rethinking the way you're doing life), believing (trusting the goodness of the Father and Jesus), and receiving the GOOD NEWS and provision of the KINGDOM (Mark 1:15). This is how one begins life from the right side of the cross.

This sounds simple, but repentance is both a human choice and a supernatural enablement (Romans 2:4). Repentance is changing the way we think and aligning with God's way of thinking. This taking-sides-with-Jesus is not merely a mental transaction; it's an act of faith that activates supernatural transformation.

SUMMARY

This series of books will unpack the epic story of **why** God (Father, Son, Holy Spirit) loves mankind so deeply; **how** He has made a way for humanity to embrace that love; and **what** living from the right side of the cross should look like for BETTER COVENANT disciples.

The first book in this series, *Seeing Through a Better Lens*, along with the upcoming books *Something New and Better* and *How to Make Sense of the Bible,* offers the vital foundation or *why* behind the series; they present a vision of NEW COVENANT living as KINGDOM OF GOD ambassadors. The next two books, *Living from the Right Side of the Cross* and *Victory on the Right Side of the Cross*, explain **how** to do **what** we were created, restored, and empowered to do as BETTER COVENANT disciples.

In short, this series of books on Living from the Right Side of the Cross is about **why** I believe **what** I believe, and **how** I live it out!

CHAPTER 1
REPENTANCE IS A GOOD WORD
Aligning with God's Way of Thinking

"The time has come, the kingdom of God has come near. Repent and believe the good news."
Mark 1:15

Have you ever made a judgment about someone based on one incident you witnessed? Then later you discovered that the incident didn't really reflect who that person is at all? We are all in process. It's just wrong to take a single freeze frame and call it a finished movie. Yet, we do it all the time, whether we realize it or not. The truth is, we are all in process. Hopefully, none of us stays exactly the same.

The journey to maturity requires continual learning, growing, and becoming. We never fully arrive. We are a work in progress.

I know I certainly don't want to stay frozen in time by the judgments of others or with some of the wrong thinking I've had in the past. Some of the things that I once held dear and would have argued for until I was red-faced, I no longer even believe.

Maturity, life experience, and a broader perspective have a way of changing one's views. For instance, when I was a 19-year-old college sophomore, I began my pursuit of becoming a wholehearted disciple of Jesus. Though I had never received any personal mentoring, I had heard enough messages on

Jesus' Great Commission to know that being a disciple of and making disciples for Jesus were at the core of His message and mandate.

So, in youthful zeal I set out to try and live a radical life for Jesus.

Surrounded by other zealous wanna-be disciples of Jesus, I was determined to live a life of radical discipline and dedication to Jesus in the setting of my college world. Truthfully, this was one of the most exhilarating seasons of my life as my band of brothers and I encountered the joy and challenges of living in community together, the honest banter of Bible discussion, the tangible presence of the Holy Spirit at our late-night prayer and worship gatherings, and the thrill of sharing the GOOD NEWS with those we came in contact with on our college campus.

As the summer of that year approached, I was invited to be the youth director of a newly started church in a nearby town. Though absolutely inexperienced, I gladly accepted this opportunity to help middle school and high school students encounter Jesus and experience His love and life that I was experiencing with my college friends.

Amazingly, the group grew from five to forty within a few months. Our unspoken strategy was simple: "Love Jesus, love each other, and then watch Him change the hearts of friends as they, too, encounter Jesus!"

We hung out together, laughed together, prayed together, had provocative conversations about the Bible together, and reached out to those who had needs or showed an interest in knowing more about Jesus.

I even occasionally worked for one of the high school guys in the youth group, who played on the local football team. He ran a hay hauling business, which is a great way to stay in shape for football season. The entire crew was made up of football players and a skinny college youth director.

At the end of each day, as we sat in the barn drinking water and recovering from a long day's work, we'd have "the talks," as they called them. Anything was fair game to discuss, and believe me, the football guys had a lot of real-life questions. Relationships were built, lives were changed, and the youth group continued to grow!

One day the lead pastor met with me to discuss the growth we were experiencing in the youth group. *"Is the group healthy?"* he asked. *"Are you making disciples?"*

I shrugged and answered unconfidently, "I think so."

He continued, *"So what are you doing to make disciples?"* I began to explain my relational, hay-field discipleship and how we were reaching young people by addressing their real-life questions with the tangible love and power of Jesus. Before I could finish, he replied, *"Oh, no! That's not discipleship! You need a measurable plan."* Then he handed me a whole stack of books that he assured me would be the best way to make disciples.

This was my introduction to organized religion.

Years later, after graduating college, getting married, and being ordained, I found myself in full-time youth ministry with a large, successful group. The only problem was I had lost my passion and zeal for ministry.

Principles and plans had replaced the Presence and Person of Jesus. Religion had been substituted for relationship. I had followed the formulas but was coming up empty. My grit, discipline, and effort to achieve a successful ministry was unfulfilling. Many times, I had thought, *"There's got to be more!"* and *"If this is all there is—I'm done!"*

I had experienced the grace of salvation, but now I needed grace to live out my salvation and its promised freedom. I desperately needed the empowering Presence of God in my life. I felt like the folks of Galatia that Paul addressed. I had begun by means of the Spirit and was now trying to finish by means of the flesh (Galatians 3:3).

Then I encountered grace!

For the next three months, grace appeared everywhere I went. It started when a friend handed me a book called *The Grace Awakening*. Another friend invited me to hear Malcolm Smith teach on grace and the NEW COVENANT. A third person introduced me to a book called *The Search for Significance*.

The shift that began to take place in my thinking was dramatic. I began to reevaluate my whole life. The most important question was no longer, *"Lord, what should I do?"* but rather, *"Lord, what do I truly believe about You, myself, and others?"*

Then on Jan. 1, 1990, as a 27-year-old Baptist youth pastor, I encountered God's grace in a very personal way. My wife Lesa and I, along with our three toddler-aged boys, traveled to Houston to attend a New Year's conference with friends at their church. The guest ministers were a husband and wife team who referred to themselves as *prophetic psalmists*. This was foreign language to me, but the love, joy, and peace that they released

Principles and plans had replaced the Presence and Person of Jesus. Religion had been substituted for relationship. I had followed the formulas but was coming up empty.

into the atmosphere when they led worship was tangible—I felt at home in Father's presence.

What was most attractive to me was how relationally and non-religiously the couple communicated the love of God. It was as if they had just had coffee with Jesus earlier and were calmly sharing His dreams and aspirations for some of His kids. Eventually, the speaker, Charles, pointed to me and said,

> "Father is freeing you from the bondage of religious constraint to be a daring deliverer of others who are entrapped and in need of His marvelous grace."

Of all the prophetic words spoken to me over that weekend nearly thirty years ago, this one message has been the constant reminder of my calling and life message. I'll also never forget Charles' parting word to me. He smiled and chuckled, and then said,

> "Here goes, I hope this makes sense to you. Papa says, 'You eat too many hotdogs.'"

The crowd laughed, but Lesa and I sat stunned. Papa certainly has a provocative sense of humor. He had confirmed His prophetic words through Charles in a simple, personal way that would make sense only to Lesa and me.

As a youth pastor, I worked late many nights. Most nights when I got home, Lesa would ask, "What would you like for supper?" I would reply, "Just make me a hotdog."

That weekend changed our lives. We purposed that we would increasingly learn how to host the presence of Father and carry His grace everywhere we went.

I was certainly in process. I was realizing that my drive to please God with my hard work, determination, and discipline was not pleasant to Him at all. In fact, it was heartbreaking to Him. I was missing the whole point of grace.

It was finally dawning on me that it is not difficult to follow Jesus—**it's impossible!** It's impossible to live a life of radical discipline and dedication to Jesus by following Him in my own strength. Being a disciple would require the grace of God Himself living in and through me.

"Father is freeing you from the bondage of religious constraint to be a daring deliverer of others who are entrapped, and in need of His marvelous grace."

My whole perspective of God and His nature needed to change. Questions abounded. Could it be that my starting point had been wrong? Could it be that the GOOD NEWS was better than I dreamed?

Could it be that Jesus had not primarily come to planet Earth because I was a bad person or a lawbreaker, but that He came because humanity had lost the plot of its story and needed to be rescued and restored to the Father and *His* story? Could it be that we as a people had forgotten who God really is and what He is truly like?

We in the West have been so indoctrinated to think of sin in legal terms—such as breaking the law— that we have missed the greater point of sin. When Jesus declared, *"No one knows the Father, but the Son"* (Matthew 11:27), He is confronting us with a much more devastating notion of sin than our Western thought even allows.

C. Baxter Kruger expounds on the deeper meaning of sin and reconciliation:

"If eternal life is 'knowing the Father,' as Jesus teaches in John 17:3, then eternal death is 'not knowing the Father' and sin is the cause of our not knowing the Father. Sin has to do with being blind and being so wrongheaded that it is impossible to know the Father. Sin goes way beyond disobedience. The deepest problem of sin is that it makes us utterly incapable of 'knowing the Father'. . . Reconciliation is not about punishment. It is about the Father reaching us in His Son in the Spirit. It is about Jesus crossing all the worlds of our confusion to establish relationship with us inside our darkness. Reconciliation is the reality that our fallen minds can be converted and we can 'know the Father' and live!"[3]

Now that's a good narrative. That's GOOD NEWS worth celebrating and sharing! That's a story of "grace that is greater than all our sin."

My view of God and myself needed to change. I needed to see through a better lens. I needed a much larger perspective of God, His purposes and His ways. I needed to repent. *Repent?* Yes, that was it. I needed to rethink my view of God and His ways.

Our entire journey to maturity with and in Christ is a journey of changing and adjusting the way we think to align with our heavenly Father.

The word *repentance* had always scared me as I pictured an angry God scolding me for not measuring up to His standard. But for the first time in my life, I was now seeing repentance as a good thing.

In one of Jesus' earliest messages, He said, *"The time has come, the Kingdom of God has come near. Repent and believe the good news"* (Mark 1:15).

I now saw it— repentance, trust, and the goodness of God all went together. The GOSPEL OF THE KINGDOM suddenly became truly "GOOD NEWS."

"Repentance is a good word," I said softly to myself. Then again a little louder, "Repentance is a great word!" Finally, I was shouting at the top of my lungs, "Repentance is a good word! Repentance is my freedom!"

The light had come on. I finally realized why Jesus had used the words *repent* and *repentance* so often. Repentance is a good word. Repentance means to change the way you think and align your thinking with God's way of thinking.

THE POWER OF PARADIGMS AND REPENTANCE

In the foreword to John MacMurray's *A Spiritual Evolution,* Paul Young shares valuable insights about paradigms and how we must be willing to see things differently in order to change the way we think (repent).

Young writes,

". . . a paradigm is a way of looking at something; it is a pair of internal glasses through which you see and apprehend the world . . . It's the grid of (your) existing beliefs that judge what it is (you) see or hear . . . We filter all our experiences though these lenses, then concretize our perceptions as truth. As a result, that which we believe to be true is as obstructed and clouded as the lens through which we see . . . Every human being sees the world, themselves and God through lenses that are crafted by genetics, experiences (both painful and wonderful), by religion (or its absence), by politics, by anger and opinion of those around, by childhood trauma, by betrayal, by exposure, by social media, by arts . . . and on and on and on . . . The impact of our paradigms is profound."[4]

I would add, the importance of repentance cannot be overstated:

- We enter into relationship with Jesus through the change called repentance.

- Our entire journey to maturity **with** and **in** Christ is a journey of changing and adjusting the way we think to align with our heavenly Father, who sees things as they really are.

- Scripture's repeated promise is that when we take sides with Jesus and change our way of thinking to align with His, it will always mean we are upgrading to the best.

At Sozo Church where I am the lead teacher, we include the following statement in our core beliefs:

"We have made a commitment to constant growth and change. We are willing to 'change our thinking' (repent) as we acquire new, clear revelation and interpretation."[5]

WHEN EVERYTHING CHANGES

Let's be honest—most of us do not like change! Change interrupts and disrupts what is familiar. Change takes us out of the normal rhythms of our lives. Change can bring anxiety, frustration, and uncertainty. But the truth is, growth and maturity cannot occur without change!

Acts 10 is the story of Cornelius, a God-seeking Roman centurion, and of Peter, a devout Jewish disciple of Jesus. The Holy Spirit orchestrates revolutionary change in each man's way of thinking by challenging generational prejudices each held.

The transformation that begins in Peter and Cornelius will ultimately affect the thinking of each man's family and society. In truth, it is still working its way through the cultures of our world today. Prejudice is a formidable stronghold. It is difficult to eradicate because it is so deeply ingrained.

When we refuse to obey God and embrace His transformation, we are actually requiring Him to repent and align with our ways.

The word *prejudice* essentially means "to pre-judge." This is what we do when we do not have all the facts or information. Prejudice is ignorance. It ignores what it does not understand. Breaking the cycle of prejudice will always require the revelation and kindness of God that leads us to repentance (Romans 2:4).

Transformational change is usually very slow and incremental. And that is certainly the case of the GOSPEL's transition from Old Covenant exclusivity (Jews only) to NEW COVENANT inclusivity (all welcome in Jesus).

When the Holy Spirit opens our eyes to fresh understanding, repentance becomes possible. The decision of what we will do with this new revelation is what we must wrestle through. So, let me ask you, how do you respond when you are with people who have different beliefs and ways than you? It's important that you are willing to wrestle with this because an open heart to all people is a major value of the KINGDOM OF GOD.

In Acts 10:1-16, God uniquely and supernaturally reveals Himself to Cornelius and Peter. God meets each person where they are. Notice the means God uses to get each person's attention: visions, trances, and angels. It seems God needs to bypass our minds to change our hearts. Sometimes our religion and tradition get in the way of the new revelation the Holy Spirit is trying to unveil to us. And like Peter, we find ourselves arguing with God, who is calling us to rethink, but we are so convinced of our way that we miss God's NEW COVENANT way completely.

As I read of Peter's argument with God in Acts 10:9-16, I find myself wondering, will Peter "get it"? Will he embrace this new revelation of the GOSPEL's inclusivity and availability for **all** to experience the love of the Father, Jesus, and Holy Spirit? Will he be able to overcome his strong ethnic, national pride and unbending racial prejudice? Will his OLD COVENANT mindset and religious tradition, passed down for more than 1,400 years, block God's new way?

Will Peter stay in his safe, comfortable, acceptable way of doing things? Or, will Peter step into God's assignment and become a world changer?

> **Peter is at a "threshold moment" in his life. This moment will define the rest of his life.**
>
> **Will Peter choose to cross over the threshold into a new way of life or play it safe? What about you?**

The truth is, if Peter accepts his mission, everything will change! So, Peter is literally wrestling in his mind with God. God is requiring Peter to repent, to align his way of thinking with His. Peter, on the other hand, is "wanting God to repent" and align to Peter's way of thinking—to keep the old ways intact. Have you ever thought of it that way?

Think back on a time you argued with or questioned God and His ways. Did this result in you hardening your heart in anger and frustration, or did it cause you to have a transformational rethink of your ideas?

So, after a surprise visit and divine encounter with three men that Cornelius had sent to fetch Peter and bring him back with them, Peter finally embraces the largeness of the GOSPEL, now available for all people. At the prompting of the Holy Spirit, Peter heads to Caesarea to meet with Cornelius, the God-seeking Gentile, and all of his Gentile family and friends.

In Acts 10:27-28 we read about the actual encounter in the home of the Gentile leader and the Jewish apostle.

> *". . . Peter went inside* [Cornelius' house] *and found a large gathering of people. He said to them: 'You are well aware that it is against our law for a Jew to associate with or visit a Gentile. But, God has shown me that I should not call anyone impure or unclean'"* (Emphasis is mine).

Put yourself in the scene. Visualize the people in the room. Feel the tension, the expectancy. Imagine the delightful surprise of Holy Spirit's powerful presence in the room. How might you have responded if you were in Peter's skin? In Cornelius' skin? One of the onlookers?

We've only scratched the surface of this incredible story. And we have not even mentioned all the supernatural aspects of spiritual transformation in the Acts 10 adventure. The rest of the story is riveting and worth reading, imagining yourself in the plot.

The truth is—we are all in the plot. We are all faced with threshold decisions, like Peter was, that will change our lives and the lives of everyone we encounter, forever.

OBSERVATIONS

🔍 Don't let your tradition, intellect, or prejudice become an obstacle that causes you to resist what God wants to do in your life by His Spirit.

🔍 God cannot be hemmed in or contained. Expect Him to speak in unusual ways and through unusual means. He will do things you don't expect, like including **all** people as His people.

🔍 God works on both sides of His initiative to bring revolutionary change. We usually wrestle and argue with God when He commands radical change.

🔍 A "threshold" experience will require active faith to cross over and step into the new revelation God is offering.

SUMMARY

Like Peter, I've had to change my way of thinking many times. I've realized that *repentance* is a good word and that aligning with Father's way of thinking is the starting point of NEW COVENANT discipleship.

I started my spiritual journey of discipleship as a 19-year-old with the wrong end game and strategy in mind. Many years later, I now realize that it is not difficult to follow Jesus—**it's impossible!**

It's impossible to live a life of radical discipline and dedication to Jesus by following Him in your own strength. This is how the life of a disciple was lived before Jesus' death on the cross, His resurrection, the coming of the Holy Spirit, and the establishment of the NEW COVENANT.

Just days before my 50th birthday I felt the Lord saying to me, "Steve, for the first two-thirds of your life you have lived in the way you understood. The last one-third of your life, I want you to trust Me to show you a better way. I want you to be willing to take big risks and change your way of thinking so you can join Me in what I have for the rest of your life."

Suddenly, the words I had received twenty-three years earlier came flooding back to my memory: *"Father is freeing you from the bondage of religious constraint to be a daring deliverer of others who are entrapped and in need of His marvelous grace."*

I now know that my assignment, for the rest of my life, is to give myself to being a daring deliverer of those entrapped by the constraint of OLD COVENANT religion. I will boldly open wide the gate to freedom and lead others on the journey to BETTER COVENANT DISCIPLESHIP!

GRACE REFLECTIONS

Jesus was brilliant at asking the *right question* to the *right person*, at the *right time*. I believe the timing of your reading of this is your *kairos* moment, a moment in time when everything changes.

1. What is God wanting to shift or change in your life?

2. What fears must be conquered in your life in order to join God in His activity in your life?

3. Are you willingly participating or resisting? (Activation means action.)

4. What does stepping over the "threshold" look like for you?

5. What first action step is the Holy Spirit impressing on your mind and heart?

CHAPTER 2
THE JESUS LENS
Seeing the Bible Through a Better Lens

"You study the Scriptures diligently because you think that in them you have eternal life. These are the very Scriptures that testify about me (Jesus), yet you refuse to come to me to have life."
John 5:39-40 (emphasis is mine)

The tragedy of Sept. 11, 2001, caused many Americans to search for the meaning of such a horrendous event. Spiritual questioning abounded. How could God allow this to happen? Was God judging America? Was God even concerned or involved at all?

It was during this time that Sam Harris, Richard Dawkins, and Christopher Hitchens burst on the scene. They became known as the new atheists. Soon the subjects of their books became the hot topics on most college campuses across America.

The heart of their message is that Christianity is dangerous! The Bible is dangerous! And as the Bible goes, so goes Christianity! In other words, if the Bible can be discredited, then the dangerous crutch called Christianity will crumble. Lest you think I'm being overly dramatic, here are a couple of quotes from Dawkins and Harris:

> "The God of the Old Testament is arguably the most unpleasant character in all fiction: jealous and proud of it; a petty, unjust, unforgiving control freak; a vindictive, bloodthirsty ethnic cleanser; a misogynistic homophobic,

racist, infanticidal, genocidal, filicidal, pestilential, megalomaniacal, sadomasochistic, capriciously malevolent bully."[6]

"The fact that my continuous and public rejection of Christianity does not worry me in the least should suggest to you just how inadequate I think your reasons for being a Christian are."[7]

I can certainly understand why the new atheists would choose to go after the Bible. All my life I had been taught that the Bible is the authoritative, inspired, inerrant, infallible Word of God that is the foundation of our faith. That's a pretty big target for sure.

But is the basic assumption of the new atheists really true? Is the Bible the right target? Is the Bible really the foundation of Christianity? Was that the view of the early church? Have the new atheists finally found the "kryptonite" that could topple the world's largest religion?

For the last few decades, church attendance in America has been in steady decline. The most rapidly growing category in most surveys is what is being called *the nones*. This is the group of persons being polled who, when asked what is their religious affiliation, check the box "none." Perhaps even more alarming is the unprecedented numbers of people who are leaving the church, saying they are done with organized religion. This growing group of people has been recently dubbed *the dones*. The *dones* leave for many reasons including church hurts and inadequate answers to heartfelt questions regarding suffering, science, social injustice, and the apparent contradictions in the Bible.

In general, people have a feeling that the church and Bible are antiquated and out of touch with their needs. Interestingly, virtually none of *the dones* are leaving the organized church because of their disinterest in Jesus.

In light of this decline, the taunts of the new atheists have had an even greater impact on some followers of Christ, causing hopelessness and fear to rise within the ranks. Is Christianity as we know it doomed? How can Christians ever turn the tide?

First, I think followers of Jesus must ask themselves some difficult questions. Is the foundation of our faith an inspired book? We paint ourselves into a corner when we make the Bible the foundation of our faith. When the Bible is our highest authority, we run the risk of committing the sin of bibliolatry, deifying the Bible itself. Make no mistake, **Jesus** is the foundation of our faith.

Before you brand me a wide-eyed liberal with a low view of Scripture, I must stop you. I have been a committed Bible reader for nearly forty years. I **love** the Bible and have a high view of Scripture. It is my constant companion. I value the Bible as a primary way that I commune with God. As a teacher, the Bible is the source for all of my teaching and preaching.

> **"The Bible is on a journey to discover Jesus, who is the living Word. If we stay on the Biblical journey, we will arrive at Jesus, who is the perfect Word of God."**
>
> **—Brian Zahnd**

The Bible and the Christian faith are closely associated, but they are not synonymous. Author and speaker Brian Zahnd lends the following insights:

"Scriptures are the soil in which the Christian faith is rooted. You cannot separate the Christian faith from the soil it's rooted in, which is the Scripture. Like a tree needs to be rooted in the soil, so the Christian faith is rooted in the Scriptures.

"The Bible doesn't stand above the story it tells, but rather it is immersed in the story it tells. The Bible is on a journey to discover Jesus, who is the living Word. If we stay on the Biblical journey, we will arrive at Jesus, who is the perfect Word of God. This is what Jesus said of Himself (John 5:39-40)."[8]

With that said, the word *Bible* simply means "books" or, more accurately, "a book of books." The Bible is a collection of inspired books, poems, letters, and Gospel accounts, among other genres of literature. A robust faith cannot be built on the defense of a book, even an inspired book. That's missing the point.

Andy Stanley says:

"I understand that the texts included in our New Testament play an important role in helping us understand what it means to follow Jesus, but they are not the reason we follow. We don't believe because of a book; we believe because of an event that inspired the book. The event, not the record of the event, is what birthed the 'church.' In other words, the Bible did not create Christianity, but rather Christianity created the Bible! The Christian faith existed for decades before there was The Bible (New Testament). Faith in Jesus existed for decades before there was The Bible (New Testament) or even Christianity!"[9] (parentheses are mine)

Second, perhaps a faith built on anything less than the Person of Jesus Himself coming to lovingly redeem and reconcile humanity is simply not a faith worth defending.

If Christianity has become merely the adherence to propositions, principles, and stories in a book, no wonder folks are leaving in droves and the atheists are having a field day dismantling it. This brand of religion has lost its heart and soul. It's lost its way. It's void of Jesus! This does not even resemble the spirit of the early church.

The Christian faith and message are about Father God reaching mankind in His Son in the Spirit. It's about Jesus crossing all the worlds of our confusion to establish relationship with us inside our darkness so that our fallen minds can be converted and we can truly "know the Father" and live!

> "...the Bible (NT) did not create Christianity, but rather Christianity created the Bible!"
>
> **—Andy Stanley**

If I were in a conversation with Sam Harris or Richard Dawkins, I believe I would share this nugget from Brian Zahnd that speaks directly to the issue of the true foundation of our faith. Zahnd writes:

"Even a casual reader of the Bible notices that between the alleged divine endorsement of genocide in the conquest of Canaan and Jesus's call for love of enemies in His Sermon on the Mount, something has clearly changed. What has changed is not God, but the degree to which humanity has attained an understanding of the true nature of God. The Bible is not the perfect revelation of God; Jesus is. Jesus is the only perfect theology. Perfect theology is not a system of theology; perfect theology is a person. Perfect theology is not found in abstract thought; perfect theology is found in the Incarnation. Perfect theology is not a book; perfect theology is the life that Jesus lived. What the Bible does infallibly and inherently is point us to Jesus, the infallible and inerrant living Word of God."[10]

So, what is the event that Stanley speaks of that "inspired the record of the event"? What event created the New Testament?

In 1 Corinthians 15:3-8 Paul declares:

"For what I received I passed on to you as of first importance: that Christ died for our sins according to the Scriptures, that he was buried, that he was raised on the third day according to the Scriptures, and that he appeared to Cephas, and then to the Twelve. After that, he appeared to more than five hundred of the brothers and sisters at the same time . . . Then he appeared to James, then to all the apostles, and last of all he appeared to me . . ."

The event that began the Jesus movement in approximately A.D. 30 has propelled the growth of the church from 25,000 followers of Jesus in A.D. 100 to 20 million followers in A.D. 310, and now to 2.3 billion Jesus followers today. That event is the Resurrection!

Over thirty years after the resurrection, Peter writes, *"Always be prepared to give an answer to everyone who asks you to give the reason for the hope that you have . . ."* (1 Peter 3:15).

Surely Peter was not saying his hope was in his Bible, for the New Testament had not even been written yet. Peter's hope was in a resurrected, living Jesus. His hope was in the relationship he had with the indwelling Christ (Colossians 1:27).

RESURRECTION SUNDAY EVENING

One of my favorite stories in the Bible is found in Luke 24:13-35. It is the story of the two disciples of Jesus on the road to Emmaus on the evening of the resurrection. This is how *The Passion Translation* relates the story:

> *13Later that Sunday, two of Jesus' disciples were walking from Jerusalem to Emmaus, a journey of about seventeen miles. 14-15They were in the midst of a discussion about all the events of the last few days when Jesus walked up and accompanied them in their journey. 16They were unaware that it was Jesus walking alongside them, for God prevented them from recognizing him.*
>
> *17-18Jesus said to them, "You seem to be in a deep discussion about something. What are you talking about, so sad and gloomy?" They stopped, and the one named Cleopas answered, "Haven't you heard? Are you the only one in Jerusalem unaware of the things that have happened over the last few days?"*
> *19Jesus asked, "What things?"*
>
> *"The things about Jesus, the Man from Nazareth," they replied. "He was a mighty prophet of God who performed miracles and wonders. His words were powerful and he had great favor with God and the people. 20-21But three days ago the high priest and the rulers of the people sentenced him to death and had him crucified. We all hoped that he was the one who would redeem and rescue Israel. 22Early this morning, some of the women informed us of something amazing. 23They said they went to the tomb and found it empty. They claimed two angels appeared and told them that Jesus is now alive. 24Some of us went to see for ourselves and found the tomb exactly like the women said. But no one has seen him."*
>
> *25Jesus said to them, "Why are you so thick-headed? Why do you find it so hard to believe every word the prophets have spoken? 26Wasn't it necessary for Christ, the Messiah, to experience all these sufferings and then afterward to enter into his glory?"*

²⁷Then he carefully unveiled to them the revelation of himself throughout the Scripture. He started from the beginning and explained the writings of Moses and all the prophets, showing how they wrote of him and revealed the truth about himself.

²⁸As they approached the village, Jesus walked on ahead, telling them he was going on to a distant place. ²⁹They urged him to remain there and pleaded, "Stay with us. It will be dark soon." So Jesus went with them into the village.

³⁰Joining them at the table for supper, he took bread and blessed it and broke it, then gave it to them. ³¹All at once their eyes were opened and they realized it was Jesus! Then suddenly, in a flash, Jesus vanished from before their eyes!

³²Stunned, they looked at each other and said, "Why didn't we recognize it was him? Didn't our hearts burn with the flames of holy passion while we walked beside him? He unveiled for us such profound revelation from the Scriptures!"

³³They left at once and hurried back to Jerusalem to tell the other disciples. When they found the Eleven and the other disciples all together, ³⁴they overheard them saying, "It's really true! The Lord has risen from the dead. He even appeared to Peter!"

³⁵Then the two disciples told the others what had happened to them on the road to Emmaus and how Jesus had unveiled himself as he broke bread with them.

THE JESUS LENS

Did you notice verse 27? It reads, *"Then he carefully unveiled to them the revelation of himself throughout the Scripture. He started from the beginning and explained the writings of Moses and all the prophets, showing how they wrote of him and revealed the truth about himself."* Jesus is declaring that He is the fulfillment of everything that Scripture is. He is the Word made flesh!

Look at verses 31-32: *"All at once their eyes were opened and they realized it was Jesus! Then suddenly, in a flash, Jesus vanished from before their eyes! Stunned, they looked at each other and said, 'Why didn't we recognize it was him? Didn't our hearts burn with the flames of holy passion while we walked beside him? He unveiled for us such profound revelation from the Scriptures!'"* Jesus reveals that He is the culmination of the Bible. He is the final, fullest revelation of God!

Once you finally see Jesus unveiled in the (Old Testament) Scriptures, everything changes. Once you see Jesus revealed as the Word made flesh, everything shifts. And once you see that Jesus is the culmination and resolution of the OLD COVENANT, you'll never read the Bible the same! You'll begin to see types and shadows of Jesus in virtually every book of the Old Testament. Perhaps for the first time in your life you will be able to make sense of the Bible.

Once you see that Jesus is the culmination and resolution of the Old Covenant, you'll never read the Bible the same!

Greater yet, you will never be the same! Now you are reading and living as Jesus prescribed—through a **Jesus Lens.** Now you're seeing Jesus as He truly is—the fullest revelation of God the Father and Scripture. The following passages are examples of this:

> *"In the past God spoke to our ancestors through the prophets at many times and in various ways, but in these last days he has spoken to us by His Son whom he appointed heir of all*

*things, and through whom also he made the universe. The Son
is the radiance of God's glory and exact representation of his
being . . . "* (Hebrews 1:1-3).

*"The Son is the image of the invisible God, the firstborn over
all creation . . . God was pleased to have all his fullness dwell
in him (Jesus), and through him reconcile to himself all
things . . . by making peace through his blood shed on a cross"*
(Colossians 1:15,19-20).

The passage that helped me see that the Jesus Lens provides
the key to understanding Scripture is in John 5. Jesus has just
healed a man at the pool of Bethesda, who had been an invalid
for thirty-eight years. You would think this would be a cause
for celebration, but not everyone is quite so happy. Because
Jesus does this miraculous act of kindness on the Sabbath, the
Jewish leaders are angry and begin to persecute Him (v.16).

John 5:17-18 says, *"In his defense Jesus said, 'My Father is
always at work to this very day, and I too am working.' For
this reason they tried all the more to kill him; not only was he
breaking the Sabbath, but he was even calling God his own
Father, making himself equal with God."*

Jesus has two strikes on Him—He has blatantly broken two
sacred rules. He has healed on the Sabbath, a real no-no for the
Jewish leaders; and worse yet, He has called God His Father.
This kind of irreverence was unheard of. He must be punished!
No, He must be killed! The situation was clearly escalating.
And what does Jesus do? Well, of course, He says, "I'm sorry
that I broke our sacred tradition. You guys are in charge, so you
must be right. How could over 1,400 years of OLD COVENANT
tradition and you angry leaders be wrong?"

Well, not exactly. Whatever image you have of Jesus while He lived on earth, you must know He was no pushover. He was not afraid to stir things up. He was constantly provoking people to rethink their positions and align with God the Father. Jesus was on a relentless mission to bring heaven to earth.

Jesus wraps up His conversation with the incensed Jewish leaders by firing one final shot at impotent religion:

"You study the Scriptures diligently because you think that in them you have eternal life. These are the very Scriptures that testify about me (Jesus), yet you refuse to come to me to have life" (John 5:39-40, with parenthesis mine).

Jesus is saying that the only way to truly make sense of the Scriptures is to read it with a Jesus Lens, because the Scriptures testify about Him. Take a look at what Brian Zahnd says in his book, *Sinners in the Hands of a Loving God*:

"The Scriptures are a means to an end, but not the end itself. If we see the Bible as an end in itself instead of an inspiring witness pointing to Jesus, it will become an idol. Idols are gods we can manage according to our own interests. If we want to make the Bible our final authority, which is an act of idolatry, we are conveniently ignoring the problem that we can make the Bible say just about whatever we want . . . the historical examples are nearly endless: crusaders, slaveholders, and Nazis have all proved their ideologies with images drawn from the Bible. Therefore, we must see the Bible as the penultimate word of God that points us to the ultimate Word of God, who is Jesus. The word *penultimate* means *almost last or next to last*. Ultimate means *final*. Jesus followers should think of Jesus first and the Bible second. The Bible is the word of God in a secondary sense, faithfully pointing to the perfect Word of God: the Word made flesh."[11]

We all have a way that we approach the Scriptures. We all have lenses through which we see life, God, and Scripture. The most effective way to "look" at the Bible is through the Jesus Lens!

John 1:14 says:

"The Word became flesh and made His dwelling among us. We have seen His glory, the glory of the one and only Son, who came from the Father, full of grace and truth."

Hebrews 4:12-13 says:

"For the word of God is alive and active. Sharper than any double-edged sword, it penetrates even to dividing soul and spirit, joints and marrow; it judges the thoughts and attitudes of the heart. Nothing in all creation is hidden from God's sight. Everything is uncovered and laid bare before the eyes of him to whom we must give account."

Read in context, it is clear that the Word of God that is alive (living) in Hebrews 4:12-13 is Jesus. He is the One to whom we must give an account (John 5:22-23).

We've got to comprehend the fact that Jesus is at the center of it all if we want to make sense of the Bible. Jesus is the living Word of God who interprets the written word of God.

PROGRESSIVE REVELATION

The Jesus Lens is a very different way to read and understand the Bible. It changes everything. It will certainly change how one sees and understands the events of the Old Testament.

Wayne Jacobsen is the first person I had ever heard use the term *Jesus Lens*. It was exactly what I needed to bring clarity and launch me into my journey of Bible exploration and discovery. Jacobsen provoked me with this question and observation: "What if God gave Israel a better religion than the one they had—to hold them in check until He could take it from them? Perhaps this is why, in the fullness of time, Jesus came to fulfill (fill full of meaning) the whole religious construct. Yet, we live as if the cross and resurrection never happened! We are new creations living in a superior covenant; why don't we believe it and live that way?"[12]

Today, many see the Old Testament as primitive and outdated. It's full of violent, bloody genocide, abuses against human rights, and killing in the name of an angry God. Unfortunately, pastors often give really weak explanations and excuses for God's bad behavior. It's an awkward dance, even for those like myself who love the Bible and believe in its inspiration.

In order for Scripture to become relevant to non-religious, thinking people in the twenty-first century, something must change! I believe that change is the reading of the Bible through a Jesus Lens.

First, we must admit that the Bible, in its writings and content, is wonderfully complex and that we do not do it justice —nor are we able to discern God's will—by simply gathering a handful of verses from various, different books of the Bible and coming up with an interpretation. If we did, we'd still be embracing slavery, polygamy, and concubinage.

Second, a systematic theology that pieces verses together around particular themes found throughout the Bible may have some value, but if this topical approach is divorced from the actual larger story the Bible is trying to convey, it will be confusing at best. It's the obvious progression to the Big Story that we must understand in order for the story to make sense.

So, how does the Jesus Lens work practically when reading and interpreting the Bible, especially troublesome passages in the Old Testament? I'm glad you asked. Let me illustrate with perhaps one of the most offensive passages in the Bible, especially to twenty-first century readers. That passage is Deuteronomy 21:10-14:

> *10When you go to war against your enemies and the Lord your God delivers them into your hands and you take captives,*
>
> *11if you notice among the captives a beautiful woman and are attracted to her, you may take her as your wife.*
>
> *12Bring her into your home and have her shave her head, trim her nails 13and put aside the clothes she was wearing when captured. After she has lived in your house and mourned her father and mother for a full month, then you may go to her and be her husband and she shall be your wife.*
>
> *14If you are not pleased with her, let her go wherever she wishes. You must not sell her or treat her as a slave, since you have dishonored her.*

Women slaves, war, slaughtered families, the taking of dead men's wives as their own brides and then casting them away if dissatisfied—what does one do with this primitive, outdated passage? Surely this should be left behind, right?

But wait . . . here's a bit of background that will explain Ancient Near East concerning the spoils of war during the period that Deuteronomy 21 was written:

"If you defeat an enemy, everything they had is now yours and they are 'objects' with which to do whatever you want. Notice, this passage is actually acknowledging women as human beings, which is a radical upgrade in a day when women were esteemed as property. The discarded brides were allowed to go free (given a certificate of divorce/legal standing), which was a great mercy, so they wouldn't have to resort to prostitution. Believe it or not, Deuteronomy 21 is actually a 'click' forward for women's rights in its day. If you read this passage today, of course it's primitive and barbaric. But if you read it as a record of what the world was like back then, and what this passage pointed toward, this is actually a giant step forward. Have we made a lot of steps forward (in regard to women's dignity, honor and rights) since then? Yes. Do we still have a long way to go? Absolutely. The Bible exists along a continuum of human growth and maturity. Though this passage looks primitive in our day, at the time it was a huge step forward."[13]

Using the Jesus Lens makes it possible to envision God's best and preferred future in even the most primitive Old Testament stories. In applying the Jesus Lens, two concepts are vital: *divine accommodation* and *progressive revelation*.

Divine accommodation simply means that God meets people where they are, not were He wishes they were.

Divine accommodation simply means that God meets people where they are, not where He wishes they were. Why? Because He is a loving Father. His love is patient and kind. He is not easily angered but rather quick to forgive. He rejoices when we discover the truth. Our heavenly Father always protects, always trusts, always hopes, always perseveres. Our Father's love for us never fails (1 Corinthians 13:4-8). Aren't you glad? I know I am.

Any parent understands this principle in raising children through the various stages of maturity. Obviously, Israel was very immature in Deuteronomy 21, having just come out of 400+ years of slavery and its accompanying slave-mindedness. The next 1,400 years would be long hard years before the coming of Jesus the Messiah and the NEW COVENANT, which would bring a whole new way of thinking and living.

Progressive revelation means that God did not unfold His entire plan to humanity in the Old Testament. The Old Testament revelation, though accurate, is incomplete. The fullness of certain teachings cannot be found in the Old Testament alone.

For instance, if I were to ask the question, "Does God require ritual blood sacrifice?" I might receive three or four different answers—all based on Scripture.

> "The priests and Levites say 'yes,' and that's what we find in the Torah. But eventually the psalmists and prophets begin to challenge this. David says, 'Sacrifice and offering You do not desire . . . Burnt offering and sin offering You have not required" (Psalm 40:6). In this psalm David contradicts the Torah's unambiguous laws requiring animal sacrifice. Later, Hosea claims that God doesn't want sacrifice but mercy (Hosea 6:6). Eventually, Jesus will weigh in to affirm the position of Hosea (Matthew 9:13; 12:7)."[14]

How can this be? Simply stated, the Bible is progressive in its revelation because God meets people where they are in their ability to comprehend His ways. If one reads the Bible in a "flat" manner, it will seem contradictory. As Brian Zahnd has said, the Old Testament Scriptures themselves are on a journey to discover Jesus. They don't stand above the story they tell but are rather immersed in the story they tell.

The things God has revealed to humanity about Himself, His purposes and His ways, were not given all at once. Why? Because the Bible is first a book written by real people, in real places at real times. That's got to be the starting point of our questions.

"Too often our questions start with 'Why did God or why didn't God . . . ?' Like, 'Why didn't God just skip the whole sacrificial system?' Well, let me ask you, 'Why didn't you skip elementary school and go directly into high school? Why didn't you skip being eight years old?' The Bible is a larger picture of you—your growth, your development, your progress. You cannot shortcut the steps in the process. So, a better question would be, 'Why did the people of that day find this story meaningful? Why did people write down that story? Why did they see need to include that poem or event?' Start at the human and you'll find yourself at the divine!"[15]

Progressive revelation means that God did not unfold His entire plan to humanity in the Old Testament.

The Old Testament revelation, though accurate, is incomplete.

God's revelation unfolded in stages as humans were ready to receive it. The ultimate revelation of God is found in Jesus Christ (Hebrews 1:3, Colossians 2:9-10).

There is a reason why Jesus chose family images as metaphors to describe what God is like. Jesus referred to God as *Father* almost exclusively. I believe the primary reason Jesus used the image of Father so frequently (over 165 times in the four Gospels) is that He wanted to illustrate that God, like a "good" human father, has incredible patience with His children in the various stages of their lives. Divine accommodation and progressive revelation in the Bible remind us that our heavenly Father always meets us where we are, no matter how immature or even deceived, and patiently leads us forward.

Jesus is the supreme example of divine accommodation and progressive revelation in the Gospels. He entered into mankind's darkness, blindness, and wrongheadedness during a time when the OLD COVENANT was what the Jewish community understood to be the full heart of God.

Jesus fired the first shots of the NEW COVENANT revolution in His Sermon on the Mount. He sent shockwaves through Judaism when He boldly declared, *"You have heard that it was said to the people long ago, 'You shall not murder, and anyone who murders will be subject to judgment,' But I tell you anyone who is angry with a brother or sister will be subject to judgment . . . "* (Matthew 5:21-22).

In the next twenty-five verses Jesus will continue this shocking mantra, "You have heard that it was said . . . but I tell you . . . !"

Can you even begin to imagine how offensive this was to His hearers? This was nothing less than a call to revolution against religion and their OLD COVENANT way of thinking and living.

If you examine Jesus' "but I say to you" statements, you'll notice that while the OLD COVENANT commandments addressed behavior, Jesus was addressing the condition of people's heart.

Jesus is harkening back to the Garden of Eden and is making a plea for restoration to Father's original intention of living a life of trust in Him as experienced in the Tree of Life. The Law, on the other hand, is an appeal to living by rules, rituals, and reason as determined by the Tree of the Knowledge of Good and Evil.

The Jesus Lens is so vitally important because it is the full revelation of God through which we see Scripture most clearly. The Jesus Lens helps us live as NEW COVENANT people, without the mixture and double-mindedness of trying to balance both the OLD and NEW COVENANT teachings simultaneously.

WHAT I AM NOT SAYING

⚠ I am not saying there are no foundational pillars of the Christian faith. God (Father, Son, Holy Spirit) are immutable, but it's our revelation of God and His ways that is growing.

⚠ I am not saying that the OLD COVENANT Law and traditions of the past have no value today. On the contrary, they provide necessary building blocks that prepare us for the fullest revelation of God in Jesus. The written Word of the Law is penultimate ("next to last"). The living Word, Jesus, is the ultimate ("the final word").

GRACE REFLECTIONS

1. Ponder this Brian Zahnd quote: "The Bible doesn't stand above the story it tells, but rather it is immersed in the story it tells. The Bible is on a journey to discover Jesus, who is the living Word. If we stay on the Biblical journey, we will arrive at Jesus, who is the perfect Word of God. This is what Jesus said of Himself (John 5:39-40)."

How does viewing the Bible as the written record of God's covenant journey with humanity change the way you read it?

2. Take a moment to read Luke 24:13-35. Crawl into the skin of the two disciples on the road. Imagine yourself having the same conversation with Jesus. What are you feeling as Jesus carefully unveils to you the revelation of Himself throughout the entire Scripture— explaining and showing you how all of the writings of Moses and the prophets actually reveal the truth about Himself (vv. 25-27)?

3. Is knowing God as revealed by Jesus your endgame when reading the Bible?

Divine accommodation simply means that God meets people where they are, not where He wishes they were. Why? Because He is a loving Father. His love is patient and kind. He is not easily angered, but rather quick to forgive. He rejoices when we discover the truth. Our heavenly Father always protects, always trusts, always hopes, always perseveres. Our Father's love for us never fails (1 Corinthians 13:4-8).

Is this your view of your heavenly Father? Do you desire to parent your own children this way?

CHAPTER 3
THE GOODNESS OF GOD
Understanding the Father Heart of God

Then Moses said, "Now show me your glory." And the Lord said, "I will cause all my goodness to pass in front of you, and I will proclaim my name the Lord, in your presence."
Exodus 33:18-19

A
s we saw in the last chapter, the Jesus Lens is vital to understanding the clearest revelation of who God is. All too often, people find themselves stuck between two polar opposite views of God. Is God kind and loving and desirous of a relationship with me, or is He angry and separated from me because of my sin? A casual reading of the Old Testament could easily leave one with the idea that God is an angry judge who demands a proper sacrifice from us in order to make Himself available.

So, which is it—loving God or angry Judge? This may seem like an impossible dilemma to sort out. Truthfully, the enormity of God, His nature and His ways, are beyond man's full understanding. In the next chapter we will look at the relationship between God and man in much greater detail when we discuss the covenant nature of God. In Luke 15, Jesus shares perhaps His most famous parable in the Bible. It's the story of two brothers and their dad. To those who grew up in church, this story is familiar. It's usually called the story of the Prodigal Son. Jesus' focus in the story, however, is not on the prodigal son but rather on the loving father.

In this chapter Jesus is communicating to two different audiences: *". . . tax collectors and sinners who had gathered to hear Jesus"* (v.1), and *"the Pharisees and teachers of the law who were muttering in the background, 'This man welcomes sinners and eats with them.'"* (v.2). What a great setting for Jesus to illustrate what the Father heart of God is truly like.

The tax collectors and sinners represent the outcasts of society. They were considered irreligious and unacceptable to God. The Pharisees and teachers of the law represent the religious experts, the spiritually elite who were "in the know."

After two brief parables about a lost sheep and a lost coin, Jesus follows with His parable of the two sons and their father. In each of these stories, the message of the Father's heart is clear: that which is lost (sheep, coin, son) is of great value. It is worth an all-out search. It is worthy of an all-out celebration.

Now Jesus goes straight to His main point in Luke 15:11-32. Hang on Pharisees and teachers of the Law: Jesus is about to blow your minds and sink your ship—which is carrying 1,400 years of reliable theology. He is going to tell a story that will let you—and the rest of society—know once and for all what God is really like! He's going to challenge the hierarchy of religion and level the playing field with grace. Take notice: God is nothing like the record-keeping, law-wielding judge that you have imagined. No! He's a loving, generous, forgiving Father.

> *[11]Jesus continued: "There was a man who had two sons. [12]The younger one said to his father, 'Father, give me my share of the estate.' So he divided his property between them.*
>
> *[13]"Not long after that, the younger son got together all he had, set off for a distant country and there squandered his wealth in wild living. [14]After he had spent everything, there was a severe*

famine in that whole country, and he began to be in need. *15So he went and hired himself out to a citizen of that country, who sent him to his fields to feed pigs. 16He longed to fill his stomach with the pods that the pigs were eating, but no one gave him anything.*

17"When he came to his senses, he said, 'How many of my father's hired servants have food to spare, and here I am starving to death! 18I will set out and go back to my father and say to him: Father, I have sinned against heaven and against you.

That which is lost is of great value. It is worth an all-out search. It is worthy of an all-out celebration.

19I am no longer worthy to be called your son; make me like one of your hired servants.' 20So he got up and went to his father. "But while he was still a long way off, his father saw him and was filled with compassion for him; he ran to his son, threw his arms around him and kissed him.

21"The son said to him, 'Father, I have sinned against heaven and against you. I am no longer worthy to be called your son.'

22"But the father said to his servants, 'Quick! Bring the best robe and put it on him. Put a ring on his finger and sandals on his feet. 23Bring the fattened calf and kill it. Let's have a feast and celebrate. 24For this son of mine was dead and is alive again; he was lost and is found.' So they began to celebrate.

25"Meanwhile, the older son was in the field. When he came near the house, he heard music and dancing. 26So he called one of the servants and asked him what was going on. 27'Your brother has come,' he replied, 'and your father has killed the fattened calf because he has him back safe and sound.'

28"The older brother became angry and refused to go in. So his father went out and pleaded with him. 29But he answered his father, 'Look! All these years I've been slaving for you and never disobeyed your orders. Yet you never gave me even a young goat so I could celebrate with my friends. ³⁰But when this son of yours who has squandered your property with prostitutes comes home, you kill the fattened calf for him!'

³¹"'My son,' the father said, 'you are always with me, and everything I have is yours. ³² But we had to celebrate and be glad, because this brother of yours was dead and is alive again; he was lost and is found.'"

ONE STORY—THREE PERSPECTIVES

I have an older brother and a younger sister. We grew up in the small South Texas town of Bloomington. Family has always been an important part of my life. As I grow older, I enjoy reminiscing about adventures we had at our grandparents' ranch, singing together as The Smothers Brothers Plus One, and reliving other childhood memories that come up in conversation. Yet, I've noticed at times that Ken, Sheryl, and I have very different perspectives on the same event from our past.

In Luke 15, Jesus offers three different perspectives on the same story. These perspectives are represented by the younger son, the older son, and the father.

Like distant memories of one's childhood, the lens through which we read Scripture is often scratched or skewed by distorted or traumatic events that occurred in our past. We all see things with a certain bias or prejudice.

Perhaps you have brothers and sisters. Chances are great that you do not have the same perspective on events from your childhood. In this story, Jesus portrays God as a good and loving Father to all. He also draws a clear comparison of the two brothers in the story with each of His two audiences: the tax collectors and sinners; and the Pharisees and teachers of the Law.

Take time to read through the story again—slowly this time. Put yourself in the skin of the younger brother, then the older brother, and finally the father. Whom do you identify with most closely in this season of your life? Now, think of a childhood event in your own life that affected you very differently than it did your brother or sister if you have siblings. Ask the Holy Spirit to show you why. What is He wanting to teach you through this? What is He wanting you to rethink?

Because our heavenly Father is better than we think, we must change the way we think! We must realign our thinking with His.

Now, let's zoom in on three important ideas we can glean from the passage: God is good; we are His children; and we have been authorized and empowered as heirs.

For years Jesus had been continuously referring to God as Father as He journeyed through Judea. Clearly, the father in this story represents God. Therefore, I will capitalize the name of Father (as well as applicable pronouns like He and His) to represent God throughout the remainder of this chapter.

GOD IS GOOD

God is incapable of being anything but good all the time! We must settle this in our minds and hearts. If not, then when difficult circumstances arise (and they will), we will be prone to blame God. The first thing I notice about the Father's goodness is that He doesn't manipulate or control us, but gives us a choice, even to make the wrong choice. True relationship demands that we have the ability to choose.

In this case, the younger son chose to exercise absolute self-centeredness. He knew what he wanted and was determined to get it. Requesting his inheritance early was tantamount to him saying, "Father, I wish You were dead. I want to take from You so I can do what I want. I want to be free and independent of You and get as far away from Your sight as possible!" This is our modern-day definition of what it means to be prodigal. So, the younger son collected his inheritance and headed for the far country, far away from his Father (Luke 15:11-19).

In Luke 15:20-24, we see the Father's response to His disrespectful, prodigal son, who by now had squandered his entire inheritance on shameful living and is returning home, smelling like pig slop and filled with shame, guilt, fear, and disgrace.

Take note, even the stench of pig-pen living cannot stop the Father's goodness and love toward His son. Filled with compassion, the Father runs to His son, throws His arms around him, kisses him, clothes him, and honors him before the entire community with an extravagant feast and celebration!

Let's unpack these verses. First, the Father is filled with compassion for His wayward son. The word *compassion* literally means "together we struggle." It pains the Father to see His son, whom He loves, live beneath his birthright and true identity.

The Father gives His son His very best. He authorizes and empowers His lost son as an heir of His KINGDOM.

Father knows and wants the best for His son, but the

son must *"come to his senses"* (v.17) and choose to return home (v.18).

Simultaneously, as the son is coming to the realization that he has been blind—wrongheaded and foolish—the Father springs into action. Father doesn't care what anyone else thinks. He doesn't care if it is seen a shame for a man over 40 to run. Father runs! And when He comes to His son, He throws His arms around His son and kisses him, and kisses him, and kisses him. He doesn't care what others think—He loves His son! He doesn't care that the community law dictates that His son should be shunned if not stoned—His beloved son is back home!

It doesn't stop there. The Father gives His son His very best. He authorizes and empowers His lost son as an heir of His KINGDOM. In Luke 15:22-24 we read:

> *22 "But the father said to his servants, 'Quick! Bring the best robe and put it on him. Put a ring on his finger and sandals on his feet. 23Bring the fattened calf and kill it. Let's have a feast and celebrate. 24For this son of mine was dead and is alive again; he was lost and is found.' So they began to celebrate."*

I'm sure that more than a few in the crowd that day might have questioned, "Why the celebration? What's so special about this reprobate boy?" One of those was the older brother. Luke 15:25-32 tells us that as he was returning from the field, he heard music and dancing. He asked a servant what was going on. "Your kid brother is home and your dad has thrown a huge party to celebrate his safe return."

The older brother got so angry that he refused to join the celebration. Interestingly, in Near Eastern culture, the oldest son's role would have been to help host and entertain the guests at such an event. So, the elder son is both angry and disobedient.

> *". . . So, his father went out and pleaded with him. ²⁹But he answered his father, 'Look! All these years I've been slaving for you and never disobeyed your orders. Yet you never gave me even a young goat so I could celebrate with my friends. ³⁰But when this son of yours who has squandered your property with prostitutes comes home, you kill the fattened calf for him!'*
>
> *³¹"'My son,' the father said, 'you are always with me, and everything I have is yours. ³²But we had to celebrate and be glad, because this brother of yours was dead and is alive again; he was lost and is found.'"*

The Father pleads for true harmony in His family. Again, we see the Father disregarding the social norm of the day, which demanded honor for the father of a household. No socially conscious father would have gone outside to *"plead"* with his disobedient older son. Instead this Father takes the road of dishonor and even shame in hopes of restoring relationship with His elder son and harmony between the two sons.

The Father appeals to the spirit, not to the mind.

The Father pleads for true harmony in His family. But, the Father's love can only be offered; it cannot be imposed.

³¹"'My son,' the father said, 'you are always with me, and everything I have is yours. ³²But we had to celebrate and be glad, because this brother of yours was dead and is alive again; he was lost and is found.'"

To the natural man this seems like foolishness or weakness, but the Father's love can only be offered; it cannot be imposed.

Earlier I mentioned that Luke 15 is one story that is seen from three different perspectives. Let's take a look at the three perspectives.

PERSPECTIVE #1

Luke 15 paints a beautiful picture of the goodness of the Father. The Father's perspective of this story is stunning. Even when we are at our worst—straight from the pig pen—He sees us as sons and daughters. Even in our religious rage, He see us as redeemable. He sees the best version of ourselves. He envisions us as the persons He created us to be. And so, He continuously woos us to *"come to our senses,"* that we may experience the NEW COVENANT life of unconditional forgiveness that He's provided. Father longs to say of each of us, *"This boy of mine was so far away from Me that he was as good as dead, but now he's alive with resurrection power! He was blind and lost, but now he is found. So there's nothing else to do but celebrate!"*

The truth is found only in the Father's perspective of your life and identity.

This is the Father's idea of our story. His perspective is that every provision has been made for our redemption and reconciliation by Jesus nearly 2,000 years ago. The only question is, will we respond to Holy Spirit's wooing and conviction and *"come to our senses"* and return to Father? Aren't you glad our heavenly Father is so good that He sees us as His kids, even at our worst? Have you experienced the lavish love of God? Do you currently describe God as extravagantly good? The truth is found only in the Father's perspective of your life and identity.

WE ARE HIS CHILDREN

One takeaway from this parable is clear but often missed. As distorted, possibly even as perverted, as our view of God may be, one thing remains constant: we are still His children. Our Father will always love us and passionately woo us with His love and kindness.

I can relate to both sons in the story. One son represents the independence of rebellion while the other represents the arrogance of religion. Both selfish independence and religious pride have distorted my perspective of my heavenly Father.

When I was 18 years old and preparing to leave home for the first time to go away to college, my dad gave me a talk that I will never forget. He said, "Your mom and I don't have much, but we have given you a name—Smothers. All I ask is that you live honorably, and don't drag that name through the mud!"

Well, I went away to school, and it quickly became my "far country." Promptly, I began to live independently, free from all restraint. And much like the younger son (which I am), I began to drag the family name through the mud.

It's interesting how my heavenly Father used other people to intersect my life and remind me of who I really was, even in my most rebellious moments when I seemed impossible to reach. One such person was an older student who would come by my dorm early each Sunday morning and invite me to go to church with him. Each Sunday I would decline. Finally, this wise friend talked to me straight: "Steve, you are probably the biggest hypocrite I know. You are trying desperately to be worse than you really are. You are a child of God; when are you gonna start living like it? When are you gonna start being who you really are?"

This was the shock that I needed. One clear call to my true identity freed me to leave the far country and come back to Father.

PERSPECTIVE #2

The younger son's perspective is influenced by blindness and wrong thinking. When he shamefully leaves his Father and goes to live in the "far country—sowing his wild oats" and choosing to distance himself from his Father—he never realizes that his Father has never left him. His Papa has never given up on him.

The biggest problem of "younger son perspective" is that, as citizens of planet Earth, we have inherited some really wrong (fallen) thinking, which has caused us to feel alienated from God. Paul explains "younger son perspective" this way:

> [21]*Once you were **alienated from God and were enemies in your minds** because of your evil behavior.* [22]*But now he has reconciled you by Christ's physical body through death to present you holy in his sight, without blemish and free from accusation* (Colossians 1:21-22–emphasis is mine).

Did you get that? Our alienation from God is in our minds. We think we are enemies with God, but it's only in our minds.

Our alienation from God is in our minds. We think we are enemies with God, but it's only in our minds.

Look at the next verse, *"but now he has reconciled you by Christ . . . you (are) holy in his sight . . . free from accusation."* Because of Jesus' death and resurrection, we are reconciled to our Father and seen as holy and free! This is why Jesus gave so much attention to repentance. We must change our thinking and align with God's thinking.

That's good news, but unfortunately the younger brother did not know who he was and how loved he was. He had a distorted view of his Father that had unnecessarily alienated him and sent him down a dead-end street. As for the tax collectors and sinners listening to Jesus, they certainly identified with the younger son. They never dreamed that they could experience the grace and love of their heavenly Father. But with Jesus' words, hope had replaced rebellion. Repentance had become a good word. Rethinking and returning to Father meant true freedom to receive His mercy, love, and grace.

PERSPECTIVE #3

I can relate to the older son also; I know the hamster wheel of religion. Having been in vocational ministry for over thirty-five years, I have often wrestled with striving and performing to please a Dad who is already pleased. I know what it's like to be angry because my religious ways of rule-keeping were just not working and I was not experiencing what the religious experts deemed "success." I, too, have been miserable, frustrated, and cranky. And as it's been said, "Misery loves company."

The formula of religious success has always been Performance + Approval. Think about it: in the OLD COVENANT, keeping all of the rules and offering an acceptable sacrifice meant you were upholding your religious obligation, and God was now happy with you. Deuteronomy 28 essentially says, "If you do good, you'll be blessed. If you do bad, you'll be cursed." This was the older son's perspective.

Jesus was offering a totally new paradigm, a foretaste of the NEW COVENANT, and it angered the Pharisees and teachers of the Law. After all, they were the experts in the Law. They were the custodians of the faith. Jesus was presenting an upside-down KINGDOM, a KINGDOM where *"mercy would triumph over judgment."* He was presenting God as a loving Father who was kind and good to all. Jesus was deconstructing their formula—no longer was Performance + Approval the way to win favor with the angry Judge.

"It can't be. It just isn't fair. What about rewarding hard work and punishing rebellion and disobedience?" The older brother wanted justice, or so he thought. Thankfully, our heavenly Father sees things differently. Even at our worst, He sees us as His kids.

Like the older son, we are often blind and confused, never even realizing that we never had to perform for Papa's approval. We've always been loved without condition. We could have had an extravagant fiesta anytime we wanted. We have immeasurable value to our Father. We are worth celebrating. We belong! These are the Father's final words:

31 "'My son,' the father said, 'you are always with me, and everything I have is yours. 32But we had to celebrate and be glad, because this brother of yours was dead and is alive again; he was lost and is found.'"

Grace is difficult to simply receive. Both of the sons have an inaccurate perspective in their stories. The younger son has worm theology—"I'm such a worm; I'm depressed beyond hope or repair." The Father's response is grace! The older son has OLD COVENANT theology—"I've got to perform harder; I've got to keep all the rules and prove I'm better than most." The only problem is, most is not the standard; Jesus is! The Father's response to his older son is grace.

Truthfully, both sons had slave mentalities. The younger son thought too poorly of himself, and the older son thought too highly of himself. One was enslaved to pity and the other to pride.

Which brother do you most relate with? What is the Holy Spirit calling you to rethink? How have you misunderstood the goodness of God in your life circumstances? Will you embrace Father's goodness? grace? unmerited and undeserved love?

One of the most difficult things for me, as a father of four grown sons, is the reality that I cannot choose for my sons. Each must choose for himself. There have been times when I have not agreed with decisions each of them has made. But before I can become judgmental, I am quickly reminded of my dad and his

Both sons had slave mentalities. The younger son thought too poorly of himself . . . The older son thought too highly of himself. One was enslaved to pity . . . the other to pride.

admonition to me as I headed off to college. I'm sure Henry Leon agonized in prayer over many of my bad decisions.

I cannot repent for my sons. We are all responsible for our own choices. Each person must respond to the voice of the Holy Spirit drawing him back to Jesus and realigning his thinking with the Father's heart and mind. Father's love can only be offered; it cannot be imposed. *"God's kindness is intended to lead us to repentance"* (Romans 2:4).

We have some tremendous advantages over the audience that originally heard Jesus' message. Why? Because we now live on the right side of the cross. Everything Jesus is pointing toward in this parable has now already been fulfilled.

Everything was accomplished in Jesus! Jesus died for the sins of humanity. As Jesus arose from the dead, He conquered death. As He ascended into heaven, everything was placed under His feet. When Jesus sat down at the right hand of Father God, He was given authority over everything in heaven and on earth. *Everything was accomplished by grace through the finished work of Jesus. It's our revelation that must grow!*

WE HAVE BEEN AUTHORIZED AND EMPOWERED AS HEIRS

Luke 15:22-24 describes the way our Father authorizes His sons (and daughters). There was no hesitancy; Father said, *"Quick, no time to waste; bring the best robe and put it on him."* This robe was a special honor of sonship. It's a new day—in your repentance and restoration to the family—and you are a new creation. The old is past; behold, all is new (2 Corinthians 5:17). *"You are no longer a slave* (a pig-pen boy)*, but God's child; and since you are His child, God has made you also an heir"* (Galatians 4:7—emphasis is mine).

The *signet ring* was also a privilege only a son could receive. It meant that this former rebel and family disgrace now had the family credit card. He had power of attorney to execute family business. Paul illustrates what NEW COVENANT partnership with the Father looks like today. *"We are therefore Christ's ambassadors, as though God were making his appeal through us . . ."* (2 Corinthians 5:20).

Next came the *sandals*, which were only for sons. Slaves and pig feeders never wore sandals—only those from wealthy families. Paul writes, *"The Spirit you received does not make you slaves, so that you live in fear again; rather, the Spirit you received brought about your adoption to sonship. And by him we cry, 'Abba, Father'"* (Romans 8:15). Those sandals were a constant reminder that he belonged to the family. He was included with all the benefits of a son.

Finally, the *barbecue feast* and *celebration* were a picture of a covenant meal. It was a demonstration to the entire community that the wayward boy, who was legally worthy of either servitude or death, was not only forgiven but being authorized and empowered as an heir. He was included in intimate family relationship.

Too often I think we miss the point regarding sin. The greatest grief of sin to the Father is that it prevents intimate relationship. Legalistic religion believes that God hates rule breakers. And truly, Father grieves when we make bad choices that leave ourselves and others wounded. But this is much too shallow a view. The greater effect of sin is that it prevents us from knowing God. It blinds and distorts so that we can no longer see the goodness of God. Sin causes a person to run and hide from God in deep shame. Sin causes us to blame God and make excuses because of our guilt. Sin paralyzes us with fear of the future and how this angry Judge of our own making will weigh our good and bad when all is said and done.

Of this much we can be certain: God is good; we are His children; and we have been authorized and empowered as heirs.

A BROADER VIEW

We have just looked through the Jesus Lens and seen His view of God as a good Father. This is the clearest revelation of God's goodness that one can get. It is the compass that keeps us on course in our discerning the heart of God when we face difficult, painful, or confusing circumstances.

Amazingly, there is currently much conflict in the church at large over the goodness of God. A major contributor is a theological position that asserts, "God is in control of everything that happens." Some in this group even believe that God is the One who causes all things to happen, good and bad.

I find this way of thinking very dangerous and divisive. Jesus said,

> *"The thief comes only to steal and kill and destroy; I have come that they may have life, and have it to the full. I am the good*

shepherd. The good shepherd lays down his life for the sheep" (John 10:10-11).

Jesus ends the debate for me! Notice a couple of things in these verses. First, Jesus says He is the Good Shepherd who has come to lovingly sacrifice His life for us that we might experience life to its fullest. Second, the thief or satan is the cause of loss, death, and destruction. It's just not that complicated: God is good, and the devil is bad. Jesus came to destroy the works of the devil (1 John 3:8). Jesus is now Lord and King and has made His believers ambassadors of His advancing Kingdom (2 Corinthians 5:20). Bill Johnson writes,

> "Many have taken the first step of discovering Jesus but tragically have stopped after step one, picking up the view of who God is as seen in the Old Testament stories. Those stories are important and necessary. But the fact is, Jesus came to replace them with a clearer view of what God is like. There are few deceptions more devastating than this one. It is tragic and so completely unnecessary."[16]

With that said, the goodness of God is clearly on display from moment one in the Old Testament. Five times in Genesis 1 the word *good* is used to describe the creation of the world and mankind. You get the idea that the very nature of God is good and that He is in a good mood. As the Bible progresses, the light of God's goodness shines brighter and brighter.

There are three prominent individuals who have an intimate relationship with God in their generation and help advance our understanding of the goodness of God. The first is Abram, whose name is later changed to Abraham.

In Genesis 12:1-3 we read:

Abraham

The Lord had said to Abram, "Go from your country, your people and your father's household to the land I will show you. I will make you into a great nation, and I will bless you. I will make your name great, and you will be a blessing. I will bless those who bless you, and whoever curses you I will curse; and all peoples on earth will be blessed through you."

Notice the goodness of God as He initiates covenant with Abram. He promises to bless Abram and his family, making them a great nation. He also promises that Abram and his descendants will be a blessing to all peoples on planet Earth. That's covenant goodness!

Through Abram (later Abraham), we learn that relationship with our good and trustworthy God is built on the foundation of faith. Abraham's name has become synonymous with faith as he is known as the father of faith and friend of God. Abraham took great risks to leave the familiarity of his home country to follow the leading of God to a Promised Land. The three great religions in our world today—Judaism, Christianity, and Islam—all trace their roots to Abraham.

The second prominent person introduced to the goodness of God is Moses. In Exodus 33:11, we learn that God spoke to Moses face-to-face as a Friend. Can you imagine being known as the guy who is God's good friend? Moses relied upon his friendship with God in the midst of very difficult circumstances. Moses' task of guiding two million Israelites from slavery in Egypt to the land promised to Abraham proves unparalleled in history.

The rest of Exodus 33 shares an incredible conversation between Moses and God.

Moses

> *12Moses said to the Lord, "You have been telling me, 'Lead these people,' but you have not let me know whom you will send with me. You have said, 'I know you by name and you have found favor with me.' 13If you are pleased with me, teach me your ways so I may know you and continue to find favor with you. Remember that this nation is your people."*
>
> *14The Lord replied, "My Presence will go with you, and I will give you rest."*
>
> *15Then Moses said to him, "If your Presence does not go with us, do not send us up from here. 16How will anyone know that you are pleased with me and with your people unless you go with us? What else will distinguish me and your people from all the other people on the face of the earth?"*
>
> *17And the Lord said to Moses, "I will do the very thing you have asked, because I am pleased with you and I know you by name."*
>
> *18Then Moses said, "Now show me your **glory**."*
>
> *19And the Lord said, "I will cause all my **goodness** to pass in front of you, and I will proclaim my name, the Lord, in your presence."* (emphasis is mine).

Wow! The glory of God is His goodness and name revealed. If this is true, then the fullest expression of God's glory is Jesus, for Hebrews 1:3 reveals that Jesus is the radiance of God's glory. Jesus is the name given to the personification of God's goodness.

The third person who experienced the goodness of God through a close personal relationship is David. In 1 Samuel 13:14 and Acts

13:22, David is called *"a man after God's own heart."* With all of his faults, David displayed the heart of God through his extravagant worship and love of God. David is a model for us today of how to reflect God's goodness:

David

   Q *Inquire of God* before making decisions.

   Q *Strengthen ourselves in the Lord* by rehearsing what He has done and promised to do.

   Q *Host the presence of God* through passionate worship.

Many of the psalms of David reflect a revelation of God that is advanced far beyond its day. His psalms are incredibly relevant today because his relationship with God reflects the heart of the NEW COVENANT goodness and nature of God.

David realized that while the goodness of God may not be fully comprehended, it can be experienced intimately. Some examples of Davidic psalms extolling the goodness of God include Psalm 34:8, where David exhorts us to *"taste and see that the Lord is good"*; and Psalm 119:68, where he declares, *"You are good and do good; teach me your statutes."*

Each of these three patriarchs of the Old Testament was in covenant with God. They had all tasted and seen the goodness of the Lord. In fact, in the first verse of the New Testament, Matthew 1:1, we read, *"This is the genealogy of Jesus, the Messiah, the son of David, the son of Abraham."* That seemingly obscure verse is the hinge point of the Old and New Testaments. Matthew is declaring that the New Testament is about the fulfillment of both the Abrahamic and Davidic covenants.

The GOSPEL, as the early church understood it, proclaims that Jesus came to fill both of these covenants full of meaning. The reality that Jesus is Lord fulfills David's covenant. The reality that Jesus was raised from the dead connects Him to the Abrahamic covenant and fills it full of meaning (Acts 2 and 3).

But what about the Mosaic covenant, the OLD COVENANT? Why is it not mentioned in Matthew 1? It's not mentioned because Jesus came to fulfill the Mosaic (Old) Covenant in a different way. According to *A Greek-English Lexicon of the New Testament, 3rd edition*, the word *fulfill* in Matthew 5:17 means "to bring to a designated end."

> *"Do not think that I have come to abolish the Law or the Prophets; I have not come to abolish them but to fulfill them."*

Jesus is saying that He did not come to abolish or destroy the credibility of the Law; He came to bring it to a designated end. Jesus resolved the dilemma of the Law and its OLD COVENANT system by forgiving and reconciling mankind to God. The coming of Jesus, the Messiah, meant the closing out of the Mosaic covenant. That is truly a demonstration of the goodness of God.

FINAL THOUGHTS

I was in fifth grade when the Jesus Movement swept through my hometown in the early 1970s. The Jesus Movement had its beginning on the West Coast of the U.S. in the late 1960s and early 1970s. It was quite revolutionary, creating a space for all types of people to worship together—around the centrality of Jesus.

It took several years for the Jesus Movement to make it to Bloomington, Texas, where I grew up—but it did. And it provided my first memories of truly vibrant church life. In the early 1970s, I couldn't wait to "go to church." The tangible presence of Jesus and the intentional exaltation of Him as Lord was captivating. Predictable church was a thing of the past.

Many in my childhood church were initially resistant to this movement. Why? Because it looked so different than predictable, traditional church. For instance, testimonies of what Jesus had done that week became regular fare. We began to sing Scripture choruses alongside cherished hymns and saw the organ phased out in favor of guitars and drums. With the influx of so many formerly unchurched teens and 20-somethings, the typical Sunday dress code became considerably relaxed.

The Jesus Movement appealed to the youth of the 1970s culture because it was real and relevant. As you might imagine, a clash erupted between long-held religious decorum and the raw, unfettered passion of newly born-again Jesus freaks or hippie types, as my Papaw called them. (Any young person with long hair and blue jeans and who played a guitar in church was a hippie to Papaw.)

The predecessor of the Jesus Movement is known as the Charismatic Movement. It had already experienced spiritual momentum for about a decade before the Jesus Movement arrived. The Charismatic Movement involves both mainline Protestant and Roman Catholic churches who regularly experience supernatural encounters, similar to those that the early church experienced in Acts. A defining tenet of the Charismatic Movement is its belief that all of the gifts of the Holy Spirit are available and normative for Christian living. Unlike the Pentecostal Movement earlier in the twentieth century, the Charismatic Movement captured the hearts of people within virtually every denomination, non-denomination, and inter-denomination.

> The KINGDOM OF GOD is a family enterprise. It is led by a loving Father who demonstrated His love by entering our darkness in the Person of the Son, Jesus. As reconciled, adopted, and restored children of God, we now display the goodness of God because His Spirit lives within us and through our lives.

The Charismatic renewal is alive and continues to expand today. The greatest numeric growth occurring in churches today, worldwide, is found predominantly in Charismatic churches.

Both the Jesus and Charismatic Movements have been used mightily to call the church back to her biblical roots of a focus on Jesus and the Holy Spirit. That's two-thirds of the Godhead, but what about a movement of the Father's heart?

In recent years (since the 2000s), there has been a stirring of what some have referred to as a Father's Love Movement. The focus of this movement is the goodness of God as our loving Father, which is the theme of this chapter. The message of the KINGDOM OF GOD and NEW COVENANT living is being restored and is beginning to capture the heart of the church.

God is sending a Tsunami of Goodness!

In August 2015, my wife and I traveled to Vacaville, California, for a School of the Prophets conference. During a prophetic encouragement session, we received a prophecy that has become a rally call of Sozo Church in San Marcos.

A couple who didn't know who we were or where we were from began sharing a powerful prophecy over Lesa and me. Suddenly, they stopped and asked us if we were pastors. We nodded in the affirmative. The funny thing is, *we were pastors of a church that did not yet exist.* Sozo Church would not form until six weeks later. Here's the basic content of the prophetic word:

> God is sending a *tsunami of goodness* to your church and region in the next five years. It will begin incrementally. The first two years will require preparation, but within that time you will begin to see pockets of God's goodness springing up. You will prepare the best you know how, but it's gonna be so good that when it gets there, you're still not gonna be prepared for how good it is.
>
> Testimonies will begin to grow, and culture will begin to change. Finally, the entire region will begin to experience this undeniable tsunami of God's goodness. Get ready . . . this will cause a major change in the way you perceive God, yourselves, and others.

As I write this, we are nearly four years into this prophesy and beginning to see the fruit of this prophesied tsunami of goodness— healings, salvations, joy, boldness, extravagant love and service— all of the gifts of the Spirit activated in the flow of people's lives and the beginning of supernatural unity in the church of the city and region.

HOW HAVE WE BEEN PREPARING FOR THIS TSUNAMI OF GOODNESS?

- We have continuously taught on the goodness of God as our loving Father within the context of a BETTER COVENANT lens.

- We have intentionally created a culture that features the kindness of the Father that leads to repentance.

- We have brought in friends, such as Charles & Marquita Patterson and Jack & Frieda Taylor, who exemplify what mature spiritual fathering and mothering look like.

- We have sought to be a family on mission—representing Jesus and our Father's goodness to the world around us.

- We have worked with other congregations in our region to create a depth of relationship and network of prayer that can steward this tsunami of goodness, transform culture in our region, and advance the KINGDOM OF HEAVEN to the ends of the earth.

WHAT I AM NOT SAYING

⚠ I am not saying that I have full and complete understanding of God. That's above any human's pay grade. If you ever get God figured out, you better get another God—yours is not big enough.

⚠ I am not saying that Father is the only metaphor or image for God in the Bible. It's just the primary description used by Jesus, who knows Him best.

⚠ I'm not saying that those who disagree with me about the goodness of God are not true believers. I'm just saying He's bigger and better than we can imagine.

GRACE REFLECTIONS

Grace is difficult to simply receive. Both of the sons have an inaccurate perspective in their stories. The younger son has **worm theology**—"I'm such a worm; I'm beyond hope or repair." The Father's response is grace! The older son has **OLD COVENANT theology**—"I've got to perform harder; I've got to keep all the rules and prove I'm better than most." The Father's response to his older son is grace!

1. Which brother do you most relate to?

2. What is the Holy Spirit calling you to rethink? How have you misunderstood the goodness of God in your life circumstances?

3. Will you embrace Father's goodness? grace? unmerited and undeserved love?

4. Can you imagine God flooding your life and the community where you live with a *tsunami of His goodness*? How might you begin to prepare in anticipation?

CHAPTER 4
A STORY OF COVENANT AND KINGDOM
With Whom Are You Agreeing?

"I am afraid that just as Eve was deceived by the serpent's cunning, your minds may somehow be led astray from your sincere and pure devotion to Christ."
2 Corinthians 11:3

Three questions are common to every person: Who am I? Who is God? And how can I step into my true identity? In this chapter, I will address the first two questions by looking at the original and lost identity of mankind in Genesis 1-3. The remainder of this book will focus on how we can step into our truest identity today.

Mankind's first question is usually *Who am I?* This is because we are so preoccupied with ourselves—our happiness, security, and purpose. The best starting point, however, is not with me; it's with understanding who God is. In the last chapter we began our journey to answering the question *Who is God?* We started with the discussion of the goodness of God. We continue that exploration by starting at the very beginning.

WHO IS GOD?

In the beginning God created the heavens and the earth . . . and the Spirit of God was hovering over the waters. And God said, "Let there be light . . ." (Genesis 1:1-3).

Notice that the creative activity of the Trinity is the focus of the Bible's first verses. God the Father is portrayed as the creative voice in verse 1. God the Holy Spirit is the breath that carries the voice in verse 2. God the Word is seen in verse 3 when He speaks the words, *"Let there be light . . ."* We later learn that Jesus is the Word of God, who becomes flesh and blood and comes to earth to be the living Word of God for mankind (John 1:1-3, 14).

The desire of God's heart has always been to bring mankind into oneness with Himself (John 17). The Trinity of God is a profound mystery that is a vital starting point for truly understanding God's eternal nature and purpose (Ephesians 1:3-14, 3:10-12).

The reality is, it took three centuries for the church to come up with a fitting image that would describe the complete nature of God. The Greek word that was chosen is *perichoresis*, which means "to dance around." *Peri* means "around;" and *choresis*, the word that choreography comes from, means "dance." Thus, God was portrayed as the Divine Dance! He is the dance or flow of life that welcomes us to enter into (their) fellowship. God is a circle of shared life between the Father and the Son in the Holy Spirit—a community of endless, mutual, giving love.

I like Dr. C. Baxter Kruger's definition of perichoresis:

"This rich and personal Greek word means *mutual indwelling* or *mutual interpenetration*. It refers to such a thorough and complete sharing of soul that the persons involved dwell in one another. The fellowship of being and life is so pure, there is union, at-oneness, and oneness (John 14:7-11). The gospel declares to us that this relationship has not ended. Jesus Christ lives now, as a human being (100% God and 100% man) in perichoretic relationship with His Father in the Spirit. The good news for us is that we have been included in this covenant (oneness) relationship in Him. It is the mission of the Holy Spirit to lead us to discover, believe, and personally participate in this relationship together. (John 14:20, 23; 17:22-26)."[17]

Though relatively few know of perichoresis today, this is the original, agreed-upon image of God by the early church. It's also the origin of the first use of the word *Trinity* to describe God.

Yes, I do know that the word *Trinity* is not found in the Bible. But what I love about this is that God is so big, He cannot be contained or explained adequately by our human languages or vocabulary. A new word that was not even in the text of Scripture had to be invented to describe the enormity of our one God in three Persons—blessed Trinity.

Maybe it's just me, but it seems like Trinity has become a bland, misunderstood, unrelatable theological term. It no longer has the beauty that perichoresis portrays. I believe it's time we recapture the loving, life-giving beauty of God. It's time that we relationally understand and embrace the God that Paul portrays in 2 Corinthians 13:14:

> *"May the grace of the Lord Jesus Christ, and the love of God (the Father), and the fellowship of the Holy Spirit be with you all."*

The grace of Jesus is a demonstrated reality (Romans 5:8). He is my freedom and purpose for living. I'm forgiven and have meaning and purpose in life because of the grace of Jesus.

The love and goodness of the Father is foundational (John 3:16-17). I receive my identity and value from my heavenly Father. I can be assured of my loving Father's protection and provision.

The fellowship of the Holy Spirit is tangible (Acts 1:8). Holy Spirit is the One who first wooed and drew me to a relationship with Jesus. She is my Comforter and ever-present Helper in times of trouble. She is my Teacher of the Scripture, Revealer of Jesus, and Source of perichoretic power.

Please don't be offended that I speak of Holy Spirit using a feminine pronoun. The truth is, no pronoun is adequate, for God is not human but "otherly." I chose the feminine pronoun for Holy Spirit because the Hebrew word "ruach" is feminine. In Genesis 1:2, the Spirit of God is portrayed as a brood hen that "broods" (hovers) over the waters. This feminine noun is used often throughout the Old Testament.

ORIGINAL IDENTITY [Who Am I?]

26Then God said, "Let us make mankind in our image, in our likeness, so that they may rule over the fish in the sea and the birds in the sky, over the livestock and all the wild animals, and over all the creatures that move along the ground."

*27So God created mankind in his own image,
in the image of God he created them;
male and female he created them.*

28God blessed them and said to them, "Be fruitful and increase in number; fill the earth and subdue it. Rule over the fish in the sea and the birds in the sky and over every living creature that moves on the ground" (Genesis 1:26-28).

Genesis 1 introduces the two major themes that thread through the entire collection of sixty-six books that make up the Bible: COVENANT and KINGDOM.

People have always had incredible worth and value in the heart of God. Genesis 1:26-27 states, twice, that mankind was created in the image and likeness of God to enjoy oneness with God. *This is our introduction to the first theme of the Bible—* COVENANT.

Covenant partnership between God and mankind is defined by relationship with Him. In the Genesis account, Adam and Eve are created to be one with God. They would rule, and He would direct.

Covenant is the way the Bible describes and defines relationship—first our relationship with God and then our relationship with everyone else. The word *covenant* means "to become one." God's desire from the beginning was that mankind would live in unfettered union with Him. He desired that, when anyone looked at humanity, they would see Him (Genesis 1:26-27). Thus, man's true identity is found in oneness with God.

Man's true identity is found in oneness with God.

The other major theme of the Bible is KINGDOM. Jack R. Taylor states,

> "A proper definition of the Kingdom must actually be twofold —the present Kingdom and the ultimate Kingdom. The ultimate, eternal Kingdom is God's rule over everything and everybody, everywhere—in eternity, past, present, and future. The present Kingdom is the emerging order of God through Christ in the affairs of humankind on earth."[18]

The KINGDOM OF GOD is the dynamic rule and reign of the Father in Christ by the power of the Holy Spirit. It must be the center of our faith and understanding of God. KINGDOM reveals our God-given responsibility and authority as His representatives on earth (Genesis 1:26, 28).

²⁶Then God said, "Let us make mankind in our image, in our likeness, so that they may rule over the fish in the sea and the birds in the sky, over the livestock and all the wild animals, and over all the creatures that move along the ground."

²⁸God blessed them and said to them, "Be fruitful and increase in number; fill the earth and subdue it. Rule over the fish in the sea and the birds in the sky and over every living creature that moves on the ground."

KINGDOM responsibility always follows COVENANT relationship because responsibility (what we do) always follows relationship (who we are). Mankind's fundamental responsibility was, and still is, to *re-present* God. One way we re-present what God is like is through the excellence and faithfulness of our work.

KINGDOM always follows covenant because what we do always follows who we are.

"The Lord God took the man and put him in the Garden of Eden to work it and take care of it" (Genesis 2:15).

Man's true identity is found in his covenant oneness with God. The overflow of that relationship is his work: re-presenting God in His KINGDOM purposes by stewarding, overseeing, and caring for all creation.

LOST IDENTITY

Adam and Eve were free to represent God in any way that was most natural to them; but God required that they depend on Him for their ethical decisions. They could eat from any tree in the Garden, including the Tree of Life. However, with all this freedom came one restriction: they were not allowed to eat from the Tree of the Knowledge of Good and Evil. The boundary was not arbitrary—it gave a framework that would set them free to enjoy their relationship with God.

Then came the event that changed everything:

GENESIS 3

> [1]*Now the serpent was more crafty than any of the wild animals the Lord God had made. He said to the woman, "Did God really say, 'You must not eat from any tree in the garden'?"*

We must understand that the serpent is by nature a deceiver, accuser, and thief. His goal is to steal mankind's true identity! His first question immediately causes the woman (Eve) to doubt and distrust God.

> [2]*The woman said to the serpent, "We may eat fruit from the trees in the garden,* [3]*but God did say, 'You must not eat fruit from the tree that is in the middle of the garden, and you must not touch it, or you will die.'"*

> [4]*"You will not certainly die," the serpent said to the woman.* [5]*"For God knows that when you eat from it your eyes will be opened, and you will be like God, knowing good and evil."*

The serpent offered Eve the fruit of the knowledge of good and evil, and told her that she would become like God if she consumed it. Notice the scheme of the serpent. He accuses God of withholding something from her. He plants a seed: "What if what you have is not enough?" And now she is just one short step to *What if I am is not enough?*

6When the woman saw that the fruit of the tree was good for food and pleasing to the eye, and also desirable for gaining wisdom, she took some and ate it. She also gave some to her husband, who was with her, and he ate it. 7Then the eyes of both of them were opened, and they realized they were naked; so they sewed fig leaves together and made coverings for themselves.

This is how satan (the adversary and accuser) steals our identity today. He lures us in with half-truths, which means they are full lies: things like, "Is God really good?" and "You are not enough!" Then he offers a counterfeit alternative that is never equal to, let alone better than, God's original offer.

The tragedy of the Fall was that, although Adam and Eve already enjoyed an unmatched relationship with God, they chose to agree with a deceptive lie (an unfounded accusation) from a disguised adversary.

This is still the issue of life. It all boils down to this question: Whom are you agreeing with? We are all listening to the voice of someone. Whose words are you agreeing with?

The consequences to that selfish betrayal were devastating! Here are five major consequences of man agreeing with the serpent's lies in the Garden. Sadly, these consequences are still rampant in our world today.

SHAME

Shame isolates and causes us to hide. Instead of running to their loving God, Adam and Eve ran from their God. Their first act after eating the forbidden fruit was to sew itchy fig leaves together to cover their nakedness. Shame was already setting in:

8Then the man and his wife heard the sound of the Lord God as he was walking in the garden in the cool of the day, and they hid from

*the Lord God among the trees of the garden. ⁹But the Lord God
called to the man, "Where are you?" ¹⁰He answered, "I heard you
in the garden, and I was afraid because I was naked; so I hid."*

How do you hear God's tone of voice when He says, "Where
are you?" Is He angry and disgusted? Or is He compassionate and
kind?

*¹¹And he said, "Who told you that you were naked? Have you
eaten from the tree that I commanded you not to eat from?"*

Is it just me, or is there a whole lot of talk about being naked?
What is that all about? First, let me say that all deception is tied to a
"perception of lack."

When God asks, "Who told you that you were naked?" He's
asking, "Who told you that you were 'lacking' something? Who
told you that I (God) am not enough to cover your needs? Who told
you that you are not enough?"

FEAR

Fear paralyzes us. We freeze. Terror, anxiety, and worry take
over. Soon our fears are totally disproportionate to reality.

Have you noticed how often your
fears don't match reality? "Wow, that
person was nothing like I had
imagined." Have you noticed how
seldom your fears ever materialize?
Most of our fears are in the future . . .
and never come to pass.

**Fear is our enemy
and must be
dealt with so we
can experience
freedom.**

Paul gives a revolutionary insight in
Colossians 1:21: "Once you were alienated from God and enemies

in your mind because of your evil behavior."

Did you get it? We are so consumed with fear, shame, and guilt in our evil behavior that we assume that God is our enemy and is alienated from us! Wow—that's distorted! But we all know what fear does to us.

Fear is our enemy. It must be dealt with so we can experience the freedom that our good and loving Father has provided for us.

> *"...I heard you in the garden, and I was afraid because I was naked (lacking); so I hid (in shame)" (Genesis 3:9—emphasis is mine).*

GUILT

Guilt causes us to make excuses and blame others. That's exactly what happens in our Genesis 3 story:

> *¹²The man said, "The woman you put here with me—she gave me some fruit from the tree, and I ate it." ¹³Then the Lord God said to the woman, "What is this you have done?" The woman said, "The serpent deceived me, and I ate."*

It's interesting to me that the three dominant world views today are Shame–Honor; Guilt–Innocence; and Fear–Power. Clearly, societies today are still influenced by Adam's sin and fall into deception.

DEATH

Death is the absence of life. Death is a futile existence in a distorted identity: distorted by its inaccurate view of God, and distorted in its view of man's purpose and priority.

Adam knows that he is dead (Genesis 2:17). He has lost his internal life and relationship with God. One day his physical body will breathe its last breath, but loss of original identity and purpose seems far worse.

What does distorted identity look like? Distorted identity finds its value in work (what I do), not in who I am: (an eikon of God), a covenant partner with Father, Son, and Holy Spirit.

SIN

Plain and simple, sin is agreeing with the devil's voice, which causes us to not know God as He really is. This will cause us to do things that are out of character with who we truly are—image-bearers of God.

Many times, we think of sin in legal terms like breaking the law. But the effect of sin is much more devastating than "missing the mark."

> . . . *23for all have sinned and fall short of the glory of God, 24and all are justified freely by his grace through the redemption that came by Christ Jesus* (Romans 3:23-24).

The greatest devastation of sin is not that we miss the mark (legally), but that by missing the mark, we miss the true "glory" of God. We fail to know who God really is. We fail to see the Divine Dance in all His glory. And because we miss the reality of who God is, we also fail to understand our truest identity as image-bearers of God.

Notice Romans 3:24. Lest we become preoccupied by sin, we should know the GOOD NEWS—we are all declared righteous by God's grace, which was demonstrated through Jesus' redeeming love.

The devastation of sin is that it distorts God's true identity and, therefore, distorts my identity. Fear is our enemy. It must be dealt with so we can experience the freedom that sin so effectively perverts, blinds, confuses, robs, and kills. Sin causes utter self-destruction because it lures us from God, which means we reject God's grace, provision, and protection.

Sin is allowed to continue in our lives because we are deceived. We don't know the truth that can set us free. So, we cope with our pain. We repeat untrue platitudes like, "I'll just have to wrestle with my sin nature until I die," as we miss the true idea behind Romans 7.

The devastation of sin is that it distorts God's true identity, and therefore distorts my identity.

Please, I beg you, back up a chapter and read the truth of the entire chapter of Romans 6. Here's a foretaste:

"Do you not know that all of us who were baptized into Christ Jesus were baptized into His death? . . . For we know that our old self was crucified with Him so that the body ruled by sin might be done away with, that we should no longer be slaves to sin— because anyone who has died (old self crucified) has been set free from sin" (Romans 6:2, 6).

Still not convinced? Read Romans 8:

"Those who live according to the flesh have their minds set on what the flesh desires; but those who live in accordance with the Spirit have their minds set on what the Spirit desires. The mind governed by the flesh is death, but the mind governed by the Spirit is life and peace" (Romans 8:5-6).

The question is, "What is your mind set on?" Or another way to say it, "Whose word are you agreeing with?"

Sin brings pain and alienates us from God (in our minds). This blindness and wrong-headedness fracture my covenant with God. Fear, shame, and guilt cause me to hide, blame, and run from my still loving, good God.

It's through agreement that the devil is able to kill, steal, and destroy.

Sin distorts the truth. God has not changed; I have. God is present and available. He's not gone anywhere. It's my sin and agreement with lies that have caused me to not know God.

Remember the words of C. Baxter Kruger,

If eternal life is "knowing the Father," as Jesus teaches in John 17:3, then eternal death is "not knowing the Father" and sin is the cause of our not knowing the Father. Sin has to do with being blind and being so wrongheaded that it is impossible to know the Father. Sin goes way beyond disobedience. The deepest problem of sin is that it makes us utterly incapable of "knowing the Father."[19]

THE POWER OF AGREEMENT

In his book *God Is Good*, Bill Johnson writes,

"Satan (the serpent) didn't come into the Garden and violently take possession of Adam and Eve. He couldn't—he had no dominion there. Because man was given the keys of dominion over earth, the devil would have to get his authority from man. The suggestion to eat the forbidden fruit was simply the devil's effort to get Adam and Eve to agree with him in opposition to God, thus empowering him. To this day it is through agreement that the devil is able to kill, steal, and destroy. He is still empowered by man's agreement.[20]

"Mankind's authority to rule was forfeited when Adam ate the forbidden fruit, for *'You are the slave of the one whom you obey'* (Rom. 6:16). In one act, mankind went from ruler over a planet, to the slave and possession of the evil one. All Adam ruled, including the title deed to the planet, became part of the devil's spoil.

"Thankfully, God's plan of redemption immediately kicked into play: 'And I will put enmity between you and the woman, and between your offspring and hers; he will crush your head, and you will strike his heel' (Gen. 3:15). Jesus would come to reclaim all that was lost."[21]

WHAT IS A COVENANT?

The power of agreement was a common understanding in Ancient Near East culture where Bible custom originates. Agreement was expressed through the cutting of a blood covenant. However, in current Western culture today, the idea of a blood covenant is not familiar. Yes, we in the West understand binding contracts, but almost entirely from a vantage of limited liability, not mutual responsibility.

An Ancient Near East covenant, like most found in the Bible, was seen as a binding agreement between two parties for the purpose of oneness. The covenants that God initiates in Scripture are called "grant covenants." They are built around the better promises of the unlimited responsibility of our God and King.

A covenant is our power of agreement with God.

The three primary covenants of the Ancient Near East that are found in the Bible are grant covenants, kinship covenants, and vassal covenants.[22] Every divine covenant in the Bible has basically three parts. Each part finds its counterpart in the Trinity of God's Person:

Words of the Covenant	⇒	The Father's Word *to us*
Blood of the Covenant	⇒	The Son's Work *for us*
Seal of the Covenant	⇒	The Holy Spirit's Work *in us*

Any covenant is incomplete and, therefore, invalid without the testimony of these three things. The triune God gave triune covenants.[23]

Recently, I have begun taking Kingdom Communion with my wife each morning. So much more than a commemorative meal, it's our daily reminder that we are in a NEW COVENANT with our heavenly Father and Jesus in the anointing of the Holy Spirit.

As we swallow the bread, we take in the goodness and all sufficiency of Christ and His covenant provision. We remember that by His stripes we are healed and made whole. As we drink of the cup, we take in the grace of our grant covenant with our Father and Savior.

Kingdom Communion reminds us of who we are! We are new creations in Christ; the old Steve, the old Lesa, have passed away. We are brand new. No, even more—we are a brand-new species!

We are covenant partners, in oneness with our Father and Savior in the anointing of their Spirit. That means we have real KINGDOM authority and power because we are in a covenant that is backed up with promises of the Father, the blood of Jesus, and the seal of the Holy Spirit.

With whom are you agreeing?

COVENANTS IN THE BIBLE

Have you ever thought, "How do I make sense of the Bible? I've tried to read it, but I just don't understand it." Well, you are not alone. I believe most intellectually honest people struggle with the Bible because they do not understand the nature of the Bible.

First, the Bible is not a single book. It is a collection of sixty-six books of various genres, written over a 1,500-year span by over forty different authors.

The clothes we wear today are a reminder of Adam and Eve's choice to abandon their true Source (the tree of Life), for self-reliance and independence (the tree of the knowledge of good and evil). Pride is always the road to destruction.

Second, *the various books that make up the Bible were not written to you, but many of them are for you and relevant to you today.* This is easily determined by learning to read Scripture with a historical, contextual interpretation.

Third, while scholars disagree on the exact number of covenants, most are in agreement that the best way to understand the Bible is to read it as the written record of God's unfolding covenant journey with humanity.[24]

I believe the first key to understanding the Bible is understanding the grand story. This is called biblical or narrative theology, as it majors on telling God's epic story of COVENANT and KINGDOM.

The following overview will help make sense of the Bible! Informed Bible readers become transformed disciples of Father and Jesus in the power of the Spirit.

In the Ancient Near East, three types of covenants were commonly created between two parties—grant covenants, kinship covenants, and vassal covenants. Understanding this information on types of covenants is worth the price of this book. If one can understand the type of covenant two parties are involved in, it will clear up many misunderstandings about the nature of God in the Old Testament.

Grant Covenant – When a king decided to honor and bless a faithful servant or a lesser king, he would establish a grant covenant. A grant covenant was the best type of covenant, because it came with no strings attached. It was unconditional and didn't require obedience on the part of the receiver. It was the generous overflow of love and grace, poured out of a ruler's heart upon the one receiving the grant covenant. (Most of the covenants in the Bible that God initiated were grant covenants.)

Kinship Covenant – When two equal parties decided to enter into covenant together, such as in a military alliance or even in marriage, this was known as a kinship covenant. This covenant came with certain obligations, which both parties would uphold, not unlike the exchanging of vows in a marriage ceremony.

Vassal Covenant – During times of war, a king may have decided to spare an enemy nation's women, children, and elderly so he could continue to exact labor and tax money from them for years to come. To keep them alive, the king would establish a vassal covenant, which was the heaviest covenant to bear. The conditions for a vassal covenant were seemingly endless, with the stipulation that if the lesser party did not uphold their end of the deal, the king would kill the rest of them.

In the Bible, we find all three of these types of covenants. The biblical text surrounding these covenants is the record (canon) of these covenants; it provides the context and culture needed to explain and make sense of the covenant.[9]

GOD'S COVENANTS WITH ADAM
📖 Genesis 1-3

God's first covenant with Adam in Genesis 1-2 occurred in the Garden of Eden before the entrance of sin. It reveals God's original purpose for mankind and mankind's original identity as image-bearers of God (Genesis 1:26-27).

God's second covenant with Adam and Eve is found in Genesis 3. It occurred after the entrance of sin. This covenant reveals the devastating effects of sin on humanity. The Adamic covenant is the result of man's lost identity because of his agreement with the serpent. This covenant prophesies the coming redemption of mankind through the Seed of woman—Jesus.

GOD'S COVENANT WITH NOAH
📖 Genesis 6-9

God's covenant with Noah occurred after the Flood. The Flood was God's judgment on the sin of mankind and the brokenness it brings. Man had not only lost his way; he had lost his entire identity and purpose in God.

This covenant is a reinstatement of God's original covenant with Adam in Eden on behalf of mankind, as well as the promise to never destroy the earth by flood (Genesis 9:11, 15). This covenant involved all of creation and all future generations. The effect of sin and rejecting God's grace is utter self-destruction. Sin kills, but God renews and gives hope of full redemption! Praise the Lord the next time you see a rainbow.

GOD'S COVENANT WITH ABRAHAM
📖 Genesis 12-50

God's covenant with Abraham is the story of a sojourner on a journey of faith. Abraham is known as the father of all who believe. This is the most comprehensive of all Old Testament covenants and the beginning of God displaying His heart to the whole world of what a family on mission looks like.

Abraham's two-step promise from God in Genesis 12 merges COVENANT *("I will bless you")* and KINGDOM *(". . . you will be a blessing to all peoples on the earth")*. The Abrahamic covenant is a grant covenant with God.

The Abrahamic covenant is referred to throughout the Old Testament, and its fulfillment in Jesus Christ is a vital part of the GOSPEL message of the early church (Acts 3:25-26).

GOD'S COVENANT WITH MOSES AND ISRAEL
📖 Exodus 19-Malachi

God's initial covenant with Moses is one of the most tragic stories in the history of Israel. It continues and magnifies the long, painful story of man's lost identity.

We pick up the story in Exodus 19. Here we see God's heart for Israel, calling her His treasured possession and offering her the opportunity to have direct access to Him through a grant covenant. God has high hopes for His children, whom He views as His KINGDOM of priests.

> *3Then Moses went up to God, and the Lord called to him from the mountain and said, "This is what you are to say to the descendants of Jacob and what you are to tell the people of Israel: 4 'You yourselves have seen what I did to Egypt, and how I carried you on eagles' wings and brought you to myself. 5Now if you obey me fully*

*and keep my covenant, then out of all nations you will be my
treasured possession. Although the whole earth is mine, ⁶you will
be for me a kingdom of priests and a holy nation.' These are the
words you are to speak to the Israelites"* (Exodus 19:3-6).

The problem, however, is that Israel does not see herself as a
royal priesthood of God. Except for Moses, who spent his
formative years in the Egyptian palace, Israel still thinks and
behaves like a band of slaves. She is a product of over 400 years of
slavery in Egypt.

After initially agreeing to God's grant covenant, Israel reneges
because of her fear of God's magnificent presence (See Exodus
19:16-19).

*²⁵But now, why should we die? This great fire will consume us,
and we will die if we hear the voice of the Lord our God any
longer . . . ²⁷(Moses) Go near and listen to all that the Lord
our God says. Then tell us whatever the Lord our God tells
you. We will listen and obey"* (Deuteronomy 5:25, 27—
emphasis is mine).

Israel's decision is the result of slave-minded fear. She does not
know the true God of her forefather Abraham. The only god(s) she
has been exposed to for over 400 years are the taskmaster gods of
Egypt. So, in a moment of irrational fear, Israel sacrifices the offer
of direct relationship with God and asks for a rulebook instead.
Rules over relationship is a bad deal.

God ultimately agrees to Israel's fearful request of a kinship
covenant, which we call the Ten Commandments, and the saddest
moment in the history of Israel is born.

Please note that the kinship covenant is Israel's idea, not an idea
of God or Moses. God offers to Moses and Israel a grant covenant

in the same way He had offered Adam, Noah, and Abraham grant covenants.

This kinship covenant is made strictly, and only, with Israel after the Exodus from Egypt to Mt. Sinai. Exodus 19-40 is the history of the forty years that followed and of Israel's repeated failure to keep the kinship covenant.

Before Moses dies and Israel enters the Promised Land, God renegotiates His covenant with her. Because of her stiff-necked rebellion and total disobedience, God downgrades the kinship covenant to a vassal covenant—which we now know as the OLD COVENANT.

In summary, the initial grant covenant that God offered Moses became a kinship covenant at the request of slave-minded Israel, and then a vassal covenant due to the repeated disobedience of Israel. What a tragic story of the lost identity of Israel and mankind!

God's simple "law of love"—called grace—became the ten laws of a kinship covenant and then 613 laws of the vassal covenant. Tragically, Israel traded relationship with God for a rulebook. For 1,400 years the rule book of the OLD COVENANT would dominate Jewish society.

GOD'S COVENANT WITH DAVID
📖 2 Samuel 7, Psalm 89; Psalm 132

The Davidic covenant is very unique. It is actually a covenant given within the timeframe of the existing Mosaic covenant. David's covenant with God will affect not only his current dynasty, but more importantly, it prophesies the kingly rule of Jesus that will come from David's lineage.

Have you ever wondered what Jewish history might have looked like if Israel had never had a king? For that matter, how would Christian history be different?

In 1 Samuel 8:5-7 we read:

5They said to him, "You are old, and your sons do not follow your ways; now appoint a king to lead us, such as all the other nations have." 6But when they said, "Give us a king to lead us," this displeased Samuel; so he prayed to the Lord. 7And the Lord told him: "Listen to all that the people are saying to you; it is not you they have rejected, but they have rejected me as their king . . ."

It seems pretty obvious that God never wanted Israel to be like other nations. He wanted her to be a *"*KINGDOM *of priests and a holy nation,"* with Himself reigning as her King.

Think about it: if there was never a human king of Israel, there would have been no King David or King Solomon. Neither would there have been a temple—just a mobile tent called a tabernacle.

Why is this important to ponder? Because kings and temples repeatedly took Israel off track in her relationship with God. Both kings and the temples they built represent Israel's desire to be just like every other nation.

In 2 Samuel 7, God initiates a covenant with King David. Notice how this KINGDOM COVENANT is closely associated with God's thoughts about the building of a temple in His honor.

2David said to Nathan the prophet, "Here I am, living in a house of cedar, while the ark of God remains in a tent." 3Nathan replied to the king, "Whatever you have in mind, go ahead and do it, for the Lord is with you." 4But that night the word of the Lord came to Nathan, saying:

5"Go and tell my servant David, 'This is what the Lord says: Are you the one to build me a house to dwell in? 6I have not dwelt in a house from the day I brought the Israelites up out of Egypt to this day. I have been moving from place to place with a tent as my dwelling. 7Wherever I have moved with all the Israelites, did I ever say to any of their rulers whom I commanded to shepherd my people Israel, Why have you not built me a house of cedar?'

8"Now then, tell my servant David, 'This is what the Lord Almighty says: I took you from the pasture, from tending the flock, and appointed you ruler over my people Israel. 9I have been with you wherever you have gone, and I have cut off all your enemies from before you. Now I will make your name great, like the names of the greatest men on earth. 10And I will provide a place for my people Israel and will plant them so that they can have a home of their own and no longer be disturbed. Wicked people will not oppress them anymore, as they did at the beginning 11and have done ever since the time I appointed leaders over my people Israel. I will also give you rest from all your enemies.

"'The Lord declares to you that the Lord himself will establish a house for you: 12When your days are over and you rest with your ancestors, I will raise up your offspring to succeed you, your own flesh and blood, and I will establish his kingdom. 13He is the one who will build a house for my Name, and I will establish the throne of his kingdom forever. 14I will be his father, and he will be my son. When he does wrong, I will punish him with a rod wielded by men, with floggings inflicted by human hands. 15But my love will never be taken away from him, as I took it away from Saul, whom I removed from before you. 16Your house and your kingdom will endure forever before me; your throne will be established forever'" (2 Samuel 7:2-16).

God is wild and free! Where He leads, we are to follow—not the other way around.

The following are a few random observations about this passage that announces the Davidic covenant:

Q God never asked anyone to build a permanent house for Him. He seems to prefer a portable tent because He is active and on the move. He doesn't want to be hemmed in by "man's prescriptions of how He should act." God is wild and free! Where He leads, we are to follow—not the other way around.

Q Contrary to David's plan, the Lord wants to build a house for David. This house will not be built with stones and mortar, but with David's descendants, who will be living stones. God wants to create a kingly covenant with David.

Q David's ruling dynasty would be fulfilled through both natural descendants and in Jesus, the King of kings.

Q About 1,000 years later, the angel Gabriel prophesies to Mary that Jesus will be the ultimate fulfillment of God's covenant with David:

"Mary, you will conceive and give birth to a son, and you are to call him Jesus. He will be great and will be called the Son of the Most High. The Lord God will give him the throne of his father David, and he will reign over Jacob's descendants forever; his kingdom will never end" (Luke 1:31-33).

Q During the last week of Jesus' life on planet Earth, the temple is Jesus' primary topic in His longest prophetic message. Jesus has no tolerance for a man-made temple, no matter how beautiful, if it is void of the presence of the living God. Jesus makes this clear in Luke 21:

[5]Some of his disciples were remarking about how the temple was adorned with beautiful stones and with gifts dedicated to God. But Jesus said, [6]"As for what you see here, the time will come when not one stone will be left on another; every one of them will be thrown down."

Q Jesus viewed the manmade temple as a distraction from the true living Temple—Himself. Kings and temples were always in God's heart, but they were to be a spiritual reality in Jesus, not man's imitation of what other nations were doing.

Q The final covenant, the NEW COVENANT, would once and for all do away with the old temple system and establish the hearts of men and women as the temples of the Spirit of God (1 Corinthians 6:19-20).

THE NEW COVENANT
📖 Jeremiah 31:31-34; Hebrews 8; Matthew 26

The NEW COVENANT is a one-of-a-kind covenant between the Father and the Son. It was made available through the cross for the entire cosmos to receive salvation. It is the single most anticipated covenant in all of Scripture. It is not only superior to the Mosaic covenant, but it fulfilled it—"bringing it to its designated end."

Through the death, resurrection, and enthronement of Jesus, the NEW COVENANT redeemed man from his sin and lostness; reconciled him to God; and restored his original created identity.

I love 2 Corinthians 5:14-6:2. This passage describes what living on the right side of the cross is all about. I will discuss this in greater detail in the next chapter, but let me give you a preview:

- We are compelled and motivated by Jesus' once-for-all death and resurrection (verses 14-15).

- Anyone who is in Christ is a new creation with a NEW COVENANT identity (verses16-17).

• God in Christ reconciled the world (cosmos) to Himself on the cross and has now committed to believers the message of reconciliation. This is the GOOD NEWS of the KINGDOM OF GOD (verses18-19).

• We have been empowered and authorized as Christ's ambassadors to spread the message of reconciliation and ministry of the KINGDOM OF HEAVEN here on planet Earth (verse 20).

• Reconciliation carries the idea of "restoration to oneness." Oneness was always God's intention for humanity: oneness with Himself in His Divine Dance, and oneness with each other. Mankind's original identity was lost (stolen) through agreement with a lie perpetuated by satan, but in time that intended identity was restored by Jesus' death and resurrection. Today our true identity in Christ is the righteousness of God (verse 21).

• *"Now is the time of God's favor, now is the day of salvation."* Today all believers live on the right side of the cross and have a restored and empowered identity in Christ (2 Corinthians 6:2).

• Remember, every divine covenant in the Bible has three parts:

Words or Promises of the Covenant
↳ The Father's Word *to us*

Blood of the Covenant
↳ The Son's Work *for us*

Seal of the Covenant
↳ The Holy Spirit's Work *in us*

- The Father's promises of the NEW COVENANT were conveyed through Jesus' saving act of forgiveness, justification, regeneration, adoption, sanctification, healing, deliverance, wholeness, etc.

- The blood of the NEW COVENANT is the once-for-all sacrifice for sin by Jesus.

- The seal of the NEW COVENANT is the Holy Spirit, who comes to live within all believers and who is the Source of our empowered identity.

SUMMARY

Understanding mankind's journey from the vantage of God's story of COVENANT and KINGDOM is absolutely vital to understanding the Bible. Grasping God's original intentions for humanity makes man's fall into deception all the more devastating.

I'm afraid that, all too often, man's objective has been to simply cope with the shame, guilt, fear, blindness, and wrong thinking we've been handed by satan and sin's deception.

It's time for God's people to stand up and boldly declare that we are free indeed!

It's time that this generation rises up and says, "**No more!**" No longer will we partner with satan's lies and accusations! No longer will we blindly agree with serpent's hiss of shame, guilt, and fear! **No more** will we accept the **lost identity** that was handed to us. It's time for God's people to stand up and boldly declare that we are **free indeed**!

Throughout the Bible story, God consistently meets man where he is and progressively releases new revelation about Himself, His purposes, and His ways.

The Divine Dance (Father in Christ in the anointing of the Holy Spirit) always knew that, in the fullness of time, He would redeem and restore man to his original identity. Mankind would finally understand what it feels like to experience true fellowship and oneness with God in Christ by the power of the Holy Spirit. Humanity would finally be a new creation with an empowered identity to advance God's KINGDOM on earth as it is in heaven.

Guess what? We are that "finally" generation! Step into your restored and empowered identity!

GRACE REFLECTIONS

In Colossians 1:21, Paul writes, *"Once we were alienated from God and enemies in our minds . . ."* Satan's primary schemes today are still deception, accusation, and lies. Because of the cross, resurrection, and enthronement of Jesus, satan's only hope is to get us to agree with his lies (especially with regard to our identity and authority).

1. With whom are you agreeing?

2. What are some specific lies regarding your identity that you have believed or agreed with? Hint: Most lies begin with the three words, "I am not" . . . good enough, worthy, loved/lovable, smart enough, beautiful/handsome, wanted, desired or desirable, important . . .

   Take time to reflect on, renounce, and repent of any serpent-inspired lies the Holy Spirit reveals to you.

3. How does agreeing with satan's lie(s) about you weaken your true authority?

CHAPTER 5
LIVING FROM THE RIGHT SIDE OF THE CROSS
Better Covenant Discipleship

"Therefore, if anyone is in Christ, he is a new creation. The old has passed away; behold, the new has come."
2 Corinthians 5:17 ESV

I am often asked, "Is disciple-making today the same as it was when Jesus walked the earth and made disciples of the original twelve?" For years my answer would have been an emphatic, "Absolutely, Jesus is our model for disciple-making, and His method is our blueprint!"

And while I still believe making disciples of all nations is our mandate from Jesus, I no longer believe that we make disciples in the same way Jesus initially did. *Why*, you ask?

Well, because we now live from the right side of the cross and enjoy all the NEW COVENANT benefits of Jesus' resurrection, ascension, enthronement, and outpouring of His Holy Spirit at the birth of His church at Pentecost. As born-again believers, we now have the Holy Spirit living inside of us.

Paul anticipated that perhaps the greatest issue for born-again believers would be that they would not know who they are and who lives within them. He wrote:

"Do you not know that your bodies are temples of the Holy Spirit, who is in you, whom you have received from God? You

are not your own; you were bought at a price. Therefore, honor God with your bodies" (1 Corinthians 6:19-20).

This may be the most revolutionary statement Paul could have made during this time in his society. It challenged over 1,400 years of deeply ingrained Jewish tradition, which believed that God resided in the Temple and was available only to a select few.

Paul was declaring that everything changed at the cross. A NEW COVENANT had been inaugurated by Jesus, and now the Father and Jesus were both available to all through the Holy Spirit.

But Paul didn't stop there. He asserted that our bodies are the dwelling place of the Holy Spirit and we can experience true fellowship and oneness with God in Christ by the power of the Holy Spirit.

Let that sink in. It's scandalous! It's total restoration to God's intended purpose for mankind.

I am one with God in Christ by the power of the Holy Spirit who lives in me! And it's all because of The Cross Event.

EMANATE NOT IMITATE

One day as I was studying 2 Corinthians 5:14-21 and pondering what NEW COVENANT discipleship looks like, this verse struck me:

> *"From now on, therefore, we regard no one according to the flesh. Even though we once regarded Christ according to the flesh, we regard Him thus no longer"* (2 Corinthians 5:16 ESV).

What is this verse saying? I believe it's saying that before Jesus died on the cross, His twelve disciples saw Him as their bearded, sandaled Jewish rabbi, whom they followed around Judea. Their goal was to do everything exactly the way Jesus did it, imitating all His ways. This was the prescribed OLD COVENANT way of discipleship.

During this transitional period, between the ending of the OLD COVENANT and the beginning of the NEW COVENANT at the cross, Jesus was simply relating with His disciples in the context and manner they understood.

The Cross Event changed everything!

Slowly and incrementally he was transitioning them out of an OLD COVENANT mindset and into a NEW COVENANT way of life.

Then Jesus was crucified. The Cross Event changed everything! The Cross Event not only split history in two—between B.C. and A.D.—but it's also the great divide of our personal existence today.

This is my translation of the apostle Paul's declaration in Galatians 6:14:

"Once you see the true greatness of what occurred on the cross, the only thing you will be able to boast in is what Christ has done for you."

On the right side of the cross, Jesus' disciples no longer view Him as their great human rabbi (2 Corinthians 5:16). They now see Jesus as the Son of God and Redeemer of all mankind! Jesus is no longer viewed as a Jewish spiritual guru or master; He is now seen as the Messiah of the world and King of all kings.

The NEW COVENANT transformed discipleship from *imitating a mentor* into *cultivating fellowship with the resurrected Jesus Christ* living in you and then *emanating Him* wherever you go (Colossians 1:27).

As new creations, we are literally a new species. We are transformed within and now have authority to live as ambassadors of Jesus and His KINGDOM everywhere we go.

Paul says it this way in 2 Corinthians 5:17, 20 ESV:

"Therefore, if anyone is in Christ, he is a new creation. The old has passed away; behold, the new has come . . . we are ambassadors for Christ, God making His appeal through us. We implore you on behalf of Christ, be reconciled to God."

I love the observation of the Fields brothers:

"It's interesting to me that we never see Paul, Peter or John quoting the words of Jesus in Matthew 28:18-20 about making disciples. The letters of the earliest believers dealt with, among other things, getting along with one another in the body of Christ. In fact, Paul never mentioned 'discipleship' in all his writings. Here's a hint: Every believer in Acts was called a disciple. Discipleship describes the way of life for ALL born again believers. Interestingly, Paul never even told anyone to 'follow' Jesus. He simply told people to put their faith in Jesus, to trust Him. Then he explained that they were **in** Christ. Paul used the terms **'In Him'** or **'In Christ'** 190 times in the New Testament, but after Matthew 28, 'discipleship' or 'making disciples' is used zero times! So, what's the point? In the new covenant, your personal relationship in Christ is more important than the stuff you do for Christ."[25]

NEW COVENANT disciples emanate the love of Jesus Christ.

As NEW COVENANT disciples, we emanate the love of Jesus Christ. Our good works are no longer a product of merely imitating Christ as best we can; they now naturally overflow from our relationship in Christ.

RIGHTEOUSNESS-CONSCIOUS NOT SIN-CONSCIOUS

Living on the wrong side of the cross is basically OLD COVENANT religion. It makes one overly sin-conscious because God is seen primarily as an angry Judge who must punish sin.

When I was in college, I was attracted to fiery preaching on sin, hell, and judgment. Why? Because through the conviction of sin, I felt the presence of God. Dan McCollam explains, "My experience through the years has been that the church has been strong in denouncing sin, but weak in presenting the truth of our new identity in Christ. Because of this, most people have a higher 'sin-consciousness' than 'God-consciousness' and are more focused on sin management than true freedom in Christ."26

> **We were created for union with God Himself. It's normal for God to dwell in us.**

In America, sin management is a multi-billion-dollar industry. Christian bookstores are full of self-help books that will teach us how to cope with and manage our sin. It's obvious that in our independent, self-reliant culture, sin management is a best-seller and our go-to prescription.

Listen to the Apostle John's thoughts in John 16:7-11:

7But very truly I tell you, it is for your good that I am going away. Unless I go away, the Advocate will not come to you; but if I go, I will send him to you. 8When he comes, he will prove the world to be in the wrong about sin and righteousness and judgment: [9]about sin, because people do not believe in me; [10]about righteousness, because I am going to the Father, where you can see me no longer; [11]and about judgment, because the prince of this world now stands condemned.

In John 16:9, John points out that Holy Spirit was sent to convict us of the sin of unbelief. But the truth is—once a person has repented of not believing in Jesus as Lord and the source of salvation—he (or she) can immediately begin his (or her) union with God in Christ by the power of the Holy Spirit.

McCollam reminds us,

"This is what we were created for, union with God Himself. It's normal for God to dwell in us. We were created for the presence of God! This is why worship lights your jets! Sadly, many believers never reach their created purpose of union; instead, they connect with God only through conviction of sin. They relate to God only on the basis of failure, shame, and guilt."[27]

This describes me as a college student. My relationship with God was based on my performance and penance. I was close to God only if I was managing my sin well or when I felt the condemnation of a fiery preacher reminding me of my shame, failure, and guilt. God was my Judge, not the loving Father I've now come to know.

Seldom does one realize where his views actually come from. For instance, St. Augustine is the most influential theologian of the West. This fourth-century, North African bishop viewed God primarily through a judicial lens. God, from Augustine's vantage, was determined to judge sin and man's inclination toward sin. Thus, Augustine's theology, which was influenced by non-Christian Greek thinkers,

Plotinus and Plato, was founded on the idea of sin-consciousness. If you have grown up in the Western church, you have been influenced by Augustine, whether you realize it or not.

Living on the right side of the cross makes one righteousness-conscious:

> *Therefore, if anyone is in Christ, he is a new creation. The old has passed away; behold, the new has come . . . For our sake he (God) made him (Jesus) to be sin who knew no sin, so that in him we might become the righteousness of God* (2 Corinthians 5:17, 21 ESV—parentheses are mine).

This was the primary position of St. Athanasius, who was born about fifty years before Augustine. Athanasius, who served as the Bishop of Alexandria, Egypt, is the most influential theologian of the East. He was the chief architect of the Nicene Creed and the major defender of the Trinity. Athanasius viewed God as Father. He got his lens of God as Father from his mentor, Irenaeus, who got his view from Polycarp, who got his lens directly from St. John himself. (See the Gospel of John for an in-depth study of Father-Son theology.)

What I believe becomes the reality I experience. So, when I fully believe that I am a new creation, literally a new species —free from my past—I am free to live out my intended identity and purpose.

Like it or not, we have all been handed a lens through which we initially view God. Unfortunately, most of us have received an inadequate or scratched lens.

Believing that I am the righteousness of God is a revolutionary game-changer. Sin-consciousness is replaced with consciousness of my true identity as righteous in Christ. No longer do I need to be preoccupied with sin management in order to satisfy God—I am the righteousness of God in Christ!

No longer do I need to play the "performance game," trying to impress an angry Judge who is scrutinizing my every move —I am the righteousness of God in Christ! No longer do I have to worry if I've not done enough or if I'm not enough—I am the righteousness of God in Christ Jesus!

> "We were created in the likeness of our Creator to manifest that which we believe to be true . . . If you believe you are separated from your Father as a Christian, you will interpret the Bible through that lens of a broken and fragile relationship. However, if you accept that you are in Him and that there is no distance, no separation between you and your Father right now, and that you can't stop the endless flood of His mercy for you, then the Bible stops being a confusing book of conflicting commandments and becomes a beautiful revelation of Love Himself."[28]

Being a new creation so powerfully reminds me of Whose I am: I'm adopted into the family of God; I'm a joint heir with Jesus; and I live by the anointing of the indwelling Holy Spirit.

Because I am in Christ and His BETTER COVENANT—I am one with God in Christ by the power of the Holy Spirit!

FORGIVENESS & THE HOLY SPIRIT

The NEW COVENANT that Israel long awaited is primarily about forgiveness and the Holy Spirit. Jeremiah 31:31-34, which was written in the 570s B.C., says,

"The days are coming," declares the Lord, "when I will make a new covenant with the people of Israel and with the people of Judah. It will not be like the covenant I made with their ancestors when I took them by the hand to lead them out of Egypt, because they broke my covenant, though I was a husband to them . . . This is the covenant I will make with the people of Israel . . . I will put my law in their minds and write it on their hearts. I will be their God and they will be my people . . . I will forgive their wickedness and will remember their sins no more."

Ezekiel prophesied for the Lord during the same time period as Jeremiah:

"I will give you a new heart and put a new spirit in you; I will remove from you your heart of stone and give you a heart of flesh. And I will put my Spirit in you and move you to follow my decrees. . ." (Ezekiel 36:26-27).

The NEW COVENANT was not simply a renewal of the old—a bit of an upgrade. No! The NEW COVENANT has made the OLD COVENANT and its way of living obsolete (Hebrews 8:13).

Forgiveness through the NEW COVENANT blood of Jesus did away with the need for sacrifices and its meticulous system. Jesus became the Perfect Sacrifice when He offered Himself for humanity's sin "once and for all." Jesus is now *"the guarantor of a better covenant"* (Hebrews 7:22). The Holy Spirit living inside of me makes going to the temple obsolete because now my body is the temple of the Holy Spirit (1 Corinthians 6:19-20).

AN ABIDING RELATIONSHIP WITH JESUS

Living from the right side of the cross is focused on cultivating an abiding relationship with Jesus. Jesus summarized the life of a NEW COVENANT disciple in this way:

"I am the vine; you are the branches. If you remain (abide) in Me and I in you, you will bear much fruit; apart from Me you can do nothing" (John 15:5—parenthesis is mine).

Fruit in this analogy is the "excess life" of Jesus flowing through you because you are in union with and indwelled by Him. What others see as the fruit of your labor, Jesus sees as the overflow of His life gushing from yours. That's guilt-free, striving-free, BETTER COVENANT discipleship. Or as Paul called it—life in Christ.

What others see as the fruit of your labor, Jesus sees as the overflow of His life gushing from yours.

. . . the fruit of the Spirit is love, joy, peace, forbearance (patience), kindness, goodness, faithfulness, gentleness, self-control. Against such things there is no law." (Galatians 5:22-23). That's the fruit of abiding in Jesus!

This difference between OLD COVENANT and NEW COVENANT discipleship proves astounding. While the OLD COVENANT focus is sin management, the NEW COVENANT focuses on our new identity as righteous in Jesus because of His finished work at the cross.

TRUSTING JESUS, NOT TRYING HARDER

Discipleship before the cross meant doing a little more and trying a little harder. It looked like striving to do better, striving to be better. Paul addresses this head on:

> *"I would like to learn just one thing from you: Did you receive the Spirit by the works of the law, or by believing what you heard? Are you so foolish? After beginning by means of the Spirit, are you trying to finish by means of the flesh?"* (Galatians 3:2-3).

These are just a few of the ways that we fall victim to striving and trying harder:

- "I die daily." (This is a misinterpretation of the meaning of 1 Corinthians 15:31 KJV.)

- Crucifying my flesh. (Galatians 2:20 says you are already crucified with Christ.)

- Managing my sin habits. (This is from a misunderstanding of Romans 7.)

- Greater self-discipline by striving to read my Bible more, pray more, fast more, love more . . . (Self-control is a fruit of the Spirit—Galatians 5:23—and spiritual practices are a means of grace, not self-effort.)

Does this sound like the life Jesus died for? This is why trusting in Jesus alone is enough:

It is for freedom that Christ has set us free. Stand firm, then, and do not let yourselves be burdened again by a yoke of slavery . . . You who are trying to be justified by the law have been alienated from Christ; you have fallen away from grace (Galatians 5:1, 4).

I have been crucified with Christ and I no longer live, but Christ lives in me. The life I now live in the body, I live by faith in the Son of God, who loved me and gave himself for me (Galatians 2:20).

This is why Jesus' death on the cross is enough to break sin's bondage:

*¹What shall we say, then? Shall we go on sinning so that grace may increase? ²By no means! We are those who have **died to sin**; how can we live in it any longer? ³Or don't you know that all of us who were baptized into Christ Jesus were **baptized into his death?***

*⁴We were therefore buried with him through **baptism into death** in order that, just as Christ was raised from the dead through the glory of the Father, we too may live a new life. ⁵For if we have been **united with him in a death like his**, we will certainly also be **united with him in a resurrection like his.** For we know that our **old self was crucified** with him so that the body ruled by sin might be done away with, that we should no longer be slaves to sin— ⁷because anyone who has died has been set free from sin. ⁸if we **died with Christ**, we believe that we will also live with him. ⁹For we know that since Christ was raised from the dead, he cannot die again; death no longer has mastery over him. ¹⁰The death he died, he died to sin once for all; but the life he lives, he lives to God. ¹¹In the same way, **count yourselves dead to sin but alive to God in Christ Jesus*** (Romans 6:1-11—emphasis is mine).

Did you get it? We have been co-crucifed with Christ and our old man is dead, dead, dead. We have been co-resurrected with Christ and our new identity screams out, "alive in Christ!" Paul wants to make sure we "get it," so he uses the word dead (to our old self) fourteen times in Romans 6:1-13. That's emphatic! My old self is dead, and I'm alive in Christ!

Discipleship on the wrong side of the cross is preoccupied with keeping every single one of the 613 laws of the OLD COVENANT perfectly. Living on the right side of the cross has only one law: the law of love.

THE LAW OF LOVE

A few years ago, I was in a beautiful park in Thessaloniki, Greece, enjoying an afternoon of sightseeing and discovering new friends. I was amazed at the diversity of people I met. A young couple who were sitting on a blanket, playing a guitar, and reading poetry were particularly interesting. Both had long dreadlocks and presented a carefree, hippy vibe. They invited me to join them, and I soon discovered they were from Israel— hitchhiking through Europe.

After about forty-five minutes of conversation, I asked if they were religious Jews. Both assured me that they were not. But after a bit of discussion, it was clear that they were very familiar with the main plot and characters of their rich spiritual history.

After a while, the girl spoke up: "The reason I would never practice the Jewish faith is because there are just too many damn rules."

I answered, "Yeah, that's why I follow Jesus. He had only one law."

There was a long pause and the girl finally said, "Okay, I'll bite—what is the one law?"

I smiled and said, "To love each other in the same way that He loved us."

Before she had time to think it through, the girl blurted out, "I could do that!"

I smiled and replied with a twinkle in my eye, "Great, would you like to follow Jesus now?"

She responded, "Oh, no! I couldn't do that." I winked, and laughter filled the air!

Discipleship from the wrong side of the cross is exhausting, with its endless rules, regulations, and rituals. Jesus said that discipleship on the right side of the cross has only one law—the law of love!

> *"A new commandment I give you: Love one another. As I have loved you, so you must love one another. By this everyone will know that you are my disciples, if you love one another"* (John 13:34-35).

Can you imagine? Only one rule— **love**! As a friend once said, Jesus seems to be saying that spiritual maturity is not based on how much you know, but on how comfortable you are with love.

BETTER COVENANT disciples are supposed to be great lovers!

Paul described Jesus' one law this way: *". . . the law of the Spirit of life in Christ Jesus has set you free from the law of sin and death"* (Romans 8:2 NASB).

Notice that the law of sin, which is OLD COVENANT sin-consciousness, is linked with death; but the law of the Spirit of life in Christ Jesus, which is NEW COVENANT righteousness-focused, is linked to freedom. Paul enlarges this thought in 2 Corinthians 3:6:

> *"He made us competent as ministers of a new covenant—not of the letter but of the Spirit; for the letter kills, but the Spirit gives life."*

Interestingly, on the day Moses came down from Mt. Sinai with the Law, 3,000 people were killed (Exodus 32:28). On the day of Pentecost when the Holy Spirit was given, 3,000 people were given new spiritual life (Acts 2:41). Truly, the letter of the law kills, and the Spirit of God gives life and freedom!

I love what Bill Vanderbush says: "If the law of the Spirit of life in Christ Jesus has set us free, then we are legally bound to be free! If Jesus was a legalist, this would be His brand of legalism: You are legally bound to be **free**—enjoy!"

Discipleship from the right side of the cross is all about freedom. It's freedom to declare:

> *"...the Son has set me free, therefore I am free indeed"*
> (John 8:36).

> *"I'm no longer a slave (to sin, fear, shame, or guilt), I am a child of God; and since I am His child, God has also made me an heir"* (Galatians 4:7—emphasis is mine).

WE ARE THE GLORY OF GOD

God's plan has always been to fill the earth with His glory (Psalm 72:19, Habakkuk 2:14). He has always desired to colonize earth with the ways of the KINGDOM OF HEAVEN. Our new life in Christ makes that dream a reality on the right side of the cross because all believers are now indwelled with the hope of glory (Colossians 1:27).

Glory is a multi-faceted word:

1. Basically, it carries the idea of magnificence, splendor, majesty, and greatness.

2. The Hebrew word for glory means "heavy or weighty," "impact or imprint." The idea is that the weight (of God) is so heavy that it leaves an imprint.

3. Another aspect of glory is the "the essence, nature, or culture of a thing."

In spring 2004, my wife Lesa and I took our four sons to New York City. We were amazed by all of the different ethnic groups represented by their own unique foods, languages, dress, and etiquette. With all of the foreign smells, sounds, and feels, I wondered, "Why are all these foreign cultures in New York?" The answer: the cultures followed the people. Another way to say it is, "the glory followed the people."

The weight of each culture was so heavy that even many years after the people left their home country, the imprint of that culture (glory) was still in them.

When the Bible says, *"The earth will be filled with the (knowledge of the) glory of God,"* it is saying the earth shall be filled with the weight of the culture of heaven. God wants earth to look and feel like heaven.

God knew if He was to bring the culture of heaven to earth, He would have to get the right species into the land. This was God's plan in the creation of mankind.

When God says, *"Let us make mankind in our image and likeness"* (Genesis 1:26), the word for image means that which is imprinted with the weight of God. So, God created a species in His own essence, nature, **glory**! In fact, mankind is the only creature that has the glory of God! Not even angels were created in God's image and likeness.

If only we understood how glorious we are. Unfortunately, most of us have no idea of our potential power. We don't know that we are the glory of God and the hope of glory for the world.

We are those created to fill the whole world with His glory.

SUMMARY

Living a BETTER COVENANT lifestyle is radically different than living by the OLD COVENANT. As we have seen, the BETTER COVENANT focuses on emanating Christ (and not the OLD COVENANT manner of imitating Christ).

While the OLD COVENANT is overly sin-conscious, the NEW COVENANT focuses on our once-for-all forgiveness and our new identity in Christ.

New life in Christ is relational while the OLD COVENANT is based on religious rules, rituals, and tradition.

The letter of the law enslaves and kills, but the Spirit gives freedom and life.

Mercy triumphs over judgment, and one law of love is superior to 613 laws of the OLD COVENANT!

In a nutshell, BETTER COVENANT discipleship is simply cultivating sensitivity to the Holy Spirit, hosting the presence of God, abiding in Jesus, being a vital part of a family on mission, and intentionally advancing the KINGDOM OF HEAVEN.

God's plan has always been to fill the earth with His glory (Psalm 72:19, Habakkuk 2:14). Our new life in Christ makes that dream a reality on the right side of the cross (Colossians 1:27).

WHAT I AM NOT SAYING

⚠ I am not saying that sin is unimportant or inconsequential. Sin is devastating because it causes us to not know God. Sin distorts, perverts, alienates, blinds, confuses our minds (Colossians 1:21), fractures our souls, and kills!

⚠ I like what Dan McCollam says: "My experience through the years has been that the church has been strong in denouncing sin, which is one of her roles, but weak in presenting the truth of our new identity in Christ. (Revisit Chapter 4 for a fuller treatment on the devastation of sin.)

⚠ I am not saying the OLD COVENANT is bad. It is merely obsolete and outdated (Hebrews 8:13). Obsolete doesn't mean bad; it means something new and better has come along—Jesus and the NEW COVENANT!

GRACE REFLECTIONS

1. What would your life be like if you had a greater God-consciousness? What if you had a greater awareness of your Father's presence, goodness, and love?

2. What would your life be like if your God-consciousness was greater than your focus on sin or shame or guilt or failure?

3. What would your life be like if you were free from having to worry about your sin and insecurity, and suddenly were released to wrestle with the greatness of your calling? and you dreams?

4. What would your life be like if your focus were no longer with your lack, but rather on the bigness of your KINGDOM-OF-GOD mission and calling?

5. If your focus were on your Kingdom mission, how much more energy would you have? How much more creativity would you have? How much more confidence would you have?

6. What if all you had to do to receive all this was just change your belief system? What if all you had to do was repent—change the way you think? How would your life be different?

PRAYER OF REPENTANCE AND ACTIVATION

Take time right now to yield up any positions that do not lead to victory, God-consciousness, or the full life Jesus died to give you. If you're on the wrong side of the cross—**admit** it, **align** with Jesus, and **pray** this prayer:

"Father, I realize that I've been living by self-effort, striving, and sometimes shame.

I repent of all unbiblical thinking and open my heart and mind to the truths of Your Word and all that Jesus accomplished through the Cross.

Lead me to an understanding of all that You have truly done for me.

I give You my whole self to this purpose. In Jesus name. Amen!"[29]

CHAPTER 6
STORIES OF THE ADVANCING KINGDOM

What's Your 'Kingdom of Heaven is Like' Story?

*". . . The kingdom of heaven is like a mustard seed . . . Though it is
the smallest of all seeds, yet when it grows, it is the largest of garden
plants and becomes a tree, so that the birds come and perch in its
branches."*
Matthew 13:31-32

"Mister, can I have forty cents?" the familiar voice requested. It had become a weekly ritual for Mike and me. Here's how it went: Smelling of alcohol, Mike would greet me on the gang-infested streets of southeast Austin and ask me for forty cents.

I would say, "Mike, I don't have forty cents to give you, but I'd be happy to buy you a hot dog and coke at the Seven Eleven."

Mike would then reply, "That's okay, I just need forty cents."

I had initially met Mike and some of his buddies while out prayer walking and scoping out the property of Crossroads Baptist Church, where I was the new pastor. While walking through the densely wooded area near the border of our property, I noticed "smoke" in the air. I rushed to see if there was an out-of-control grass fire. To my amazement, I discovered it was a campfire. But it was more than just a camp fire; it was the home of Mike, Reggie, and Charlie.

As I wandered into their camp, I was welcomed and invited to join them for a drink and some cold spam. I respectfully declined. (At 10 in the morning, neither was very appealing). We sat on some old tree stumps and visited in their "living room." After a while, Mike asked, "What kind of business are you in?"

Trying to be discrete, I answered "I'm in the 'GOOD NEWS' business."

Mike pondered a second and then said, "Oh, you're our new preacher. Me and the guys were wondering when we were gonna get a new preacher."

Tentatively I asked, "Do you attend the services at Crossroads?"

In unison they replied, "No, but we can hear the music every Sunday here at the camp and join in on the songs we know."

What happened next was surreal. Charlie asked me if I knew "Amazing Grace." Then, sort of embarrassed, he said, "Well, of course you do; would you mind singing with us?" So, there I was out in the middle of the woods, singing "Amazing Grace" at 10 a.m. with a bunch of half-drunk, homeless men. Not exactly how I had planned to spend my morning, but I must confess, the whole ordeal was exhilarating. I felt incredibly alive there in the woods with Mike, Charlie, and Reggie.

Over the next two years we would become good friends. Though none of them ever attended a Sunday worship service, I truly became their pastor and they my congregation. We just "congregated" at their camp instead of the facility that bore the name Crossroads.

Often, I would drop by while out prayer walking the neighborhood. Sometimes they'd walk along with me. Other times we'd sit around their campfire and visit. Occasionally, we'd sing together or read from the Bible. Always, they would ask me to pray for them and the dangerous neighborhood they lived in.

Though some of the leadership at Crossroads did not like Mike, Charlie, and Reggie "living in the woods on our property," my appeal was always, "What do you think Jesus would do?" These men deserved some dignity and care. Life on the streets is hard and dangerous. On more than one occasion each of them had been beaten up and robbed. Cautiously, the leadership team acquiesced to my appeal, but with the firm warning to please be careful.

PLEASE PRAY FOR ME

One day, Mike approached me, and before he could say anything, I said, "Sorry, Mike, I don't have forty cents, but I'd be happy to buy you a hotdog and a drink (Coca-Cola, that is)." To my surprise, Mike said he was not there for money this time. He had come to ask for prayer.

Mike continued, "My life is a mess. I know that I'm drinking myself to death." He held out his trembling hands before me. "I can't stop shaking. My life is a wreck, and I really want help this time."

Mike had anticipated my line of questioning. A few times over the past couple of years we had talked about his alcohol problem. I had prayed for his deliverance, but to no avail. Each time, Mike would sober up for a few days, but when circumstances got rough, he'd return to the familiarity and security of the bottle. He said, "If you'll just pray for me, I promise I'll do my part and stay sober." So reluctantly, I placed my hand on his shoulder and began to pray. As the words came out of my mouth, an electric shock passed between us, and Mike found himself lying on the ground about six or seven feet away. As he stumbled to his feet, I invited him to come inside the church building. We both knew that God was up to something powerful.

Over the next several minutes, Mike cried out to God. He confessed his sin, anger, and bitterness over past failures and the events that had brought such hurt into his life. He welcomed Jesus Christ into his life to be his Savior and new Master. He renounced the idol of alcohol that had served as the illegitimate source of his security for so many years. When Mike finished praying, he looked up at me—and he was radiant.

For the next several weeks, Mike became my right-hand man. He'd come up to the church and help with yard work. We'd visit and discuss his progress and goals for the future. Overall, Mike was doing incredibly well.

Then, as suddenly as he had appeared in my life, Mike disappeared. I searched the "camp," but neither Charlie or Reggie knew where he had gone. I asked the locals around the neighborhood, but nobody knew Mike's whereabouts.

I THINK MIKE IS DEAD

About three months later, on a Wednesday night during a leadership team meeting, I heard a knock on the front door of the church. It was Charlie, and he was very emotional. He had been drinking heavily and was difficult to understand. So, I told him that I would visit with him after my meeting. When the meeting was over, Charlie was nowhere to be found, so I went home.

The next morning when I arrived at the church, Charlie was there waiting for me. He apologized for not meeting with me the night before and confessed that he had passed out on a bench. Quickly he came to the point: "I think Mike is dead. I think he was run over last night while trying to cross Stassney Lane."

I was shocked. "Are you sure? How can we find out?"

Charlie informed me that Mike's elderly parents lived just a few blocks away. "They would know," Charlie said. By now Reggie had walked out of the woods and had joined our conversation.

The three of us loaded up in my old Chevy Impala and headed for Mike's parents' home. When we got there, the worst was confirmed. Mike's elderly mom told us that Mike had been hit by a truck as he crossed the highway the night before. Reggie, Charlie, and I sat there and cried together as we mourned the loss of our friend.

When Mike's mom found out that I was a pastor, she invited me to the viewing of Mike's body at the funeral home later that evening. I had no idea what was about to transpire in the next forty-eight hours.

I arrived at the funeral home that evening and discovered that Mike had grown up in the Catholic church and the plan was that he be buried in a Catholic cemetery. However, there seemed to be some sort of controversy about whether he was a "Catholic in good standing" and qualified to be buried in the Catholic cemetery.

WHAT HAPPENED TO MIKE?

While Mike's mom was discussing these details with the Catholic priest, I met the rest of the family. Interestingly, two of Mike's sisters were committed Christ-followers, and one sister told me that she was a graduate of a ministry school in Tulsa. After a wonderful conversation, one of Mike's sisters asked me if I would speak at Mike's funeral the next day. I told her I would be honored. Then she looked at me intently and asked, "What happened to Mike? When he moved back in with Mom and Dad a few months ago, he was different. He had stopped drinking. He was always talking about what Jesus had done for him. What happened to Mike?"

My heart thrilled as some of the missing pieces to the puzzle of Mike's disappearance had been discovered. As I shared the story of Mike's salvation and miraculous deliverance, tears of gratitude filled the eyes of both of Mike's sisters.

THE FUNERAL

By the next day, I had accumulated yet another to take with me to Mike's funeral: Charlie, Reggie, and Leo. Leo was my Guatemalan friend who attended Crossroads Church. On this day I needed all the support I could get, particularly since the Mass portion of the funeral would be conducted in Latin. I would need Leo to help interpret as best he could.

Our motley crew arrived at the funeral home, and I immediately dropped the guys off and met with the Catholic priest, who had agreed to conduct the funeral. Our meeting was brief, very brief. He looked at me and said, "You have five minutes, and only five minutes—at the graveside." That was it. Our conversation was over, and he walked into a back room for "clergy only." I was escorted to the auditorium where the service was to be held.

Earlier that day, as Charlie, Reggie, Leo, and I drove to the funeral home, it occurred to me that we might be the only friends Mike had, other than his family. I mean, how many friends could a homeless man have? I had braced myself for the worst.

When the usher opened the auditorium door, I was shocked. Most of the funeral home auditorium was full. (In fact, Leo, Reggie, Charlie, and I had to sit on the back row.)

As it turned out, Mike had been a successful businessman earlier in his life, but the loss of his wife had caused him to turn to alcohol. The constant "numbing out" on alcohol had caused Mike to lose his business, family, friends, and self-respect. Eventually, he wound up hopeless, homeless, and in utter despair.

When the service began, I leaned over to Leo and asked, "What is the priest saying?" (He was speaking in Latin.)

Leo responded, "Brother Steve, I don't know all he's saying, but I can tell you he's not preaching the GOSPEL." Throughout the service I would receive updates from Leo, "He's still not preaching the GOSPEL."

Finally, we arrived at the graveside. After some preliminary remarks, the priest nodded at me to come forward and share. As I approached, he said quietly under his breath, "Remember, you have only five minutes." He had made my parameters clear. What could I share that would have any significant impact in just five minutes?

THE KINGDOM OF HEAVEN IS LIKE . . .

As I stood in front of Mike's casket, I simply described my meeting with Mike a few months earlier. I detailed the God encounter that had occurred in Mike and his intentional, heartfelt commitment to the Lordship of Jesus Christ:

> "Years of counseling, rehab, and therapy could not produce the results of that one spontaneous encounter with God," I said.
>
> "The Kingdom of heaven is like a homeless man who appeared outwardly to be insignificant, whose life seemed to be wasted," I continued. "Yet after encountering Jesus, the Pearl of great price, he recognized that he, too, was of great value. Mike's life mattered, because he found the One who really matters and gives meaning to life. Through Mike, I've learned that the Kingdom of heaven is like the impact of the life of a homeless man.
>
> "Come to think of it, wasn't the man who had the greatest eternal impact on history a homeless man during the last years of His life?"

After my five-minute "KINGDOM OF HEAVEN Is Like" story, I invited anyone who would like to commit their life to Christ, like Mike did, to meet with me for prayer later. As I stepped away from the casket so the priest could continue, I was stunned by what happened next. A young lady came forward and stood in front of me for prayer. As I put my hand on her shoulder, she fell to her knees.

After praying with her to receive Christ as her Savior, I looked up and noticed a line forming behind her. And Mike's mom was the first in line. She and I both sensed the uneasiness of the priest, so she suggested that the "prayer line" be directed to her house immediately following the graveside service. She boldly declared, "This man will be at my house and will pray for anyone with need."

JESUS COMES TO MIKE'S HOUSE

As Leo, Charlie, Reggie, and I made our way to Mike's parent's home, we shared fond memories of Mike. Leo asked if we could go by the church to pick up a few Spanish Gospel-tracts. He added, "You never know, Brother Steve, there may be someone who wants to know Jesus—and the language of heaven is Spanish." (It was also the language of most of Mike's family and friends.)

By the time we arrived at Mike's parents' home, many friends and family had already gathered. Food was being served inside the house, and most of the men gathered outside to drink a cold Corona and visit under the shady oak trees in the front yard.

Charlie and Reggie blended into the sea of people while Leo and I were ushered into the bedroom of Mike's bed-ridden dad. Mike's two sisters and mom were already there, waiting on us. After a time of prayer, we left the room and entered the kitchen, where most of the people were serving themselves homemade tortillas and brisket.

I was handed a paper plate and got in line for a hot tortilla, when a 16-year-old girl approached me. She said, "I have been going to church all my life, but today is the first time I've ever really understood what it means to give my life to Jesus."

I inquired, "Have you ever entrusted your life to Christ?"

With tears streaming down her face, she said, "No, but I would like to."

Moments later she and I prayed a simple prayer of faith: "Jesus, I need you in my life. By your grace, I trust you with me. I receive your love and forgiveness. Be Lord of my life–beginning now."

The next couple of hours were incredible. Leo was in his element, sharing the GOOD NEWS of the KINGDOM OF GOD with most of the men under the shade trees as I wandered around looking for someone who spoke English.

Vera, who worked at a laundromat in the neighborhood, sought me out. She said that she was touched by what had happened in Mike's life. She explained how her son was embattled in a struggle with alcohol, drugs, and an immoral lifestyle. "Would you go to my son's house and pray for him? Today I have new hope for him."

As we drove to Vera's son's home, I thought to myself, "Who would have ever imagined the opportunities that have opened up today. And all because of a 'KINGDOM OF HEAVEN Is Like' story at the funeral of a homeless man."

Jesus said,

"Then the King will say to those on his right, 'Come, you who are blessed by my Father; take your inheritance, the kingdom prepared for you since the creation of the world. For I was hungry and you gave me something to eat, I was thirsty and you gave me something to drink, I was a stranger and you invited me in, I needed clothes and you clothed me, I was sick and you looked after me, I was in prison and you came to visit me.'

"Then the righteous will answer him, 'Lord, when did we see you hungry and feed you, or thirsty and give you something to drink? When did we see you a stranger and invite you in, or needing clothes and clothe you? When did we see you sick or in prison and go to visit you?'

"The King will reply, 'I tell you the truth, whatever you did for one of the least of these brothers of mine, you did for me'" (Matthew 25:34-40).

JESUS HAD ONLY ONE SERMON

Jesus of Nazareth was certainly the most captivating teacher who ever walked the face of the earth. His creativity was unparalleled. He was the master storyteller who could keep the attention of large crowds of men, women, and children for hours.

But perhaps the most interesting thing about Jesus was that He essentially had only one message or theme. Sure, He had hundreds of illustrations and applications, but if you invited Jesus to speak at your town, you were going to get His central message: The KINGDOM OF GOD or the KINGDOM OF HEAVEN, terms He used interchangeably.

> **Jesus came to establish KINGDOM OF GOD on earth as it is in heaven... He came to be God's ruling presence.**

The whole reason Jesus came to earth was to establish the KINGDOM OF GOD on earth as it is in heaven (Matthew 6:10). He did not come to earth to merely proclaim the doctrine of the KINGDOM OF GOD; rather He came to be the manifestation of God's ruling presence.

Jesus began His ministry with these revolutionary words:

"The time is fulfilled, the Kingdom of God is at hand, repent, and believe in the gospel" (Mark 1:15 NASB).

Unfortunately, to our twenty-first century, GOSPEL-saturated ears, this sounds rather bland and familiar, even religious. To first-century hearers, this proclamation was the most radical pronouncement anyone had ever dared to make.

In *The Secret Message of Jesus*, Brian McLaren gives some detail to the background and setting into which Jesus arrived. Jesus was born into a Jewish family and society, and primarily ministered to Jewish people. He was raised under the constant oppression of Roman occupation. Actually, Israel had been occupied by foreign rulers for over six hundred years.

"When Jesus arrived on the scene," McLaren writes, "four major groups had emerged as the philosophical leaders in Israel. First, there were the Zealots who believed that violence and force was the answer to everything. 'The reason we're oppressed is that we're passive and cowardly. If we would have courage, if we would rise up and rebel, God would give us victory. If we would take action and slit a few Roman throats, if we had the faith to launch a violent revolution, God would give us power, like David, to defeat the Goliath that is Rome so we would be free.'

"A second group, the Herodians, named for supporters of the puppet ruler, Herod, strongly disagreed. 'You have no idea how powerful Rome is. To rebel is suicide. Resistance is futile; they would crush us.'[30]

"Another group, the Essenes, felt the only way to get God's approval was to leave the mainstream of society and retreat to the desert in a kind of monastic lifestyle of holiness. Society was beyond hope and must be abandoned altogether.

"A fourth group, the Pharisees, said the problem was sin and lack of purity. God would deliver the Jews, once again, 'If there were more righteous people like us and fewer sinners among us—fewer prostitutes, drunks, and Roman collaborators

—then Roman domination would be brought to an end by God. Religious purity and rigor—that's the answer!'"

Trying to fit Jesus into one of these four boxes was futile, though certainly most first-century listeners probably tried. His message of the KINGDOM OF GOD was revolutionary, yet He did not fit the physically violent mold of the Zealots. He was clearly not a Herodian or Essene—not a "go with the flow" or "get out of Dodge" kind of guy. I'm sure initially, many thought, "I bet he's a Pharisee." That kind of thinking didn't last long as Jesus began to confront head-on the hypocritical, lifeless, manmade traditions of the Pharisees.

As McLaren states,

"Jesus seems to be a bundle of contradictions. You can't stop wondering about him, trying to figure Him out. You get out to hear Jesus every chance you can . . . you ask people you know to summarize His message. Eventually it becomes clear: this man is not just another revolutionary; He is calling for a revolutionary new sort of revolution. You've never heard anything like it, and you are both attracted and unsettled."[31]

Clearly, Jesus began His ministry with an explosive blast: "Get ready, the time has come, there's a new King in town, with a new way of doing things. This **Jesus was a** King won't change His ways to **"show and tell"** accommodate you, so you had better **Messiah.** repent (change your way of thinking) and enter into a trust relationship with Him and His way of governing."

Though never specifically defined, the government of God on earth, it appears, was generally demonstrated by Jesus in two ways: by *"doing the works of his Father"* (John 4:34) and by *"destroying the works of the devil"* (1 John 3:8).

Throughout His ministry, Jesus instructed His disciples to declare and demonstrate the GOSPEL of the KINGDOM. Jesus was a "show and tell" Messiah. When He sent out the twelve (and later the seventy-two), He said,

"As you go, preach this message: 'The Kingdom of heaven is near.' Heal the sick, raise the dead, cleanse those who have leprosy, and drive out demons. Freely you've received, freely give" (Matthew 10:7-8).

The proclamation and demonstration of the KINGDOM OF GOD was central to Jesus' purpose and mission while on earth:

JESUS' FIRST MESSAGE	"The time has come, the KINGDOM OF GOD has come near. Repent and believe the GOOD NEWS." ↳ *Mark 1:15*
JESUS' MODEL PRAYER	"Your KINGDOM come, Your will be done, on earth as it is in heaven." ↳ *Matthew 6:10*
JESUS' TEACHING	Designed to show men how they might enter the KINGDOM OF GOD. ↳ *Matthew 5:20; 7:21*
JESUS' MIGHTY WORKS	Intended to prove that the KINGDOM had come upon them. ↳ *Matthew 12:28*
JESUS' PARABLES	Illustrated to His disciples the truth about the KINGDOM. ↳ *Matthew 13*

JESUS' CENTRAL MISSION	That the GOSPEL OF THE KINGDOM would be preached in the whole world. ↳ *Matthew 24:14*
JESUS' FINAL MESSAGE	A "show and tell" teaching centered around the message of the KINGDOM OF GOD. ↳ *Acts 1:3*
HIS DISCIPLES' MESSAGE & MISSION	Jesus and the KINGDOM OF GOD! ↳ *Acts 8:12; Acts 19:8; Acts 28:30-31*

THE KINGDOM OF HEAVEN IS LIKE . . .

One of my favorite chapters in the Bible is Matthew 13. I love it because Jesus is trying to teach His twelve disciples about His favorite topic: the KINGDOM OF HEAVEN.

It becomes even more fascinating when you frame the setting the way the scholar of Hebrew studies Dr. Ray Vander Laan does. Vander Laan says, "There is some evidence that ten of Jesus' disciples were 15 to 16 years old, while John, who was youngest, may have been as young as 10 years old. Simon Peter, who was married or at least had a mother-in-law, was the oldest disciple. He was probably in his early 20s."[32]

Do you get the picture? Here are "possibly" ten teenage boys, a pre-teen, and a 20-something listening to Jesus' profound parables about the KINGDOM OF HEAVEN. They are trying to "get it." They truly want to be like their leader and understand this all-important message that seems to consume Jesus.

In Matthew 13, Jesus gives eight rapid-fire parables that illustrate what the KINGDOM OF HEAVEN is like. He starts out with the Parable of the Sower and the four different types of soil. You can almost hear Him say, "You gotta get this one; you'll not understand all the other parables if you don't get this one! Do you get it?"

He quickly moves to the second parable, *"The Kingdom of heaven is like a man who sowed good seed in his field . . ."* Next Jesus says, *"The Kingdom of heaven is like a mustard seed . . . Yes, and it's also like yeast . . . "* Then He declares, *"The Kingdom of heaven is like treasure hidden in a field . . . It's like a merchant looking for fine pearls, until he has found the one pearl of great value, and then he goes away and sells everything he has and buys it."*

In the seventh parable Jesus states, *"The Kingdom of heaven is like a net that was let down into the lake and caught all kinds of fish . . . "* The KINGDOM is incredibly diverse! It's not a "Jews only" social club. If fact, it's a mixed bag. Like the variety of fish you pull up from the sea, you'll be amazed at the types the KINGDOM draws in.

Finally, Jesus says the KINGDOM OF HEAVEN is like the owner of a house who brings out of his storeroom new treasures as well as old.

By now, Jesus is wildly impassioned as He has poured out His heart, expounding on and illustrating the deep truths of His favorite topic to His spiritual sons and protégées. I love the next verse, *"Jesus said to them (disciples), 'Have you understood all these things?' They said to Him, 'Yes, Lord'"* (Matthew 13:51— parenthesis is mine).

This reminds me of viewing the vacation pictures of an exuberant friend who's just come back from New York: "Here's a picture of the outside of Yankee Stadium. Here's a view from inside Yankee Stadium. This is a picture of the west bleachers of Yankee Stadium. This is snapshot shows the infield of Yankee Stadium."

After a while, you say, "Okay, I get it—Yankee Stadium."

Now, I wasn't there with Jesus and His twelve, but I used to work with 15-year-olds every week. If these 15-year-olds were like my posse, I'm sure they "didn't get it." But I love this passage because it illustrates Jesus' patience with us until we do get it.

One of the main things I think Jesus wants us to "get" is the reality that the dynamic rule of God can be illustrated in virtually an infinite number of ways. He was giving His boys a few snapshots of what the KINGDOM OF HEAVEN is like.

GET YOUR OWN STORIES

I believe Jesus never intended that we merely sit around regurgitating His stories and parables of what the KINGDOM is like. Instead, He desires that we tell our own fresh "KINGDOM OF HEAVEN is like" stories from our daily encounters with Him and the many ways we bring the reality of His KINGDOM to others and they to us. We all have KINGDOM OF GOD stories that need to be in circulation. So, get your own stories!

I believe nothing is more powerful in building our faith and the faith of others than sharing current "KINGDOM OF GOD is like" stories. At Sozo Church, we call them "Yay, God!" stories. From day one, sharing "Yay, God!" stories has been a major component of our church culture. At every senior leader meeting, core team meeting, leadership rally, Life Group, dinner party group, equipping event, etc., we spend the first portion of our time together sharing "Yay, God!" and "KINGDOM OF HEAVEN is like" stories.

Why? Because thanksgiving, gratitude, and testimony of what God is doing creates a NEW COVENANT/KINGDOM environment. In virtually every gathering, beginning with praise of God's past goodness and blessing, it quickly turns into real-time prophecy. Why? Because the testimony of Jesus is the Spirit of prophecy and *". . . it is the Spirit of prophecy who bears testimony to Jesus"* (Revelation 19:10).

We all have KINGDOM OF GOD stories that need to be in circulation. So, get your own stories!

The Hebrew word for testimony is "ehud," which literally means "witness" or "record." In our legal system, if a crime is committed and someone sees it, they then give testimony in a courtroom of what they saw. Their testimony is a witness or record of what happened.

The root word also means "to duplicate or repeat." Combining the two thoughts, we should repeatedly make known what God has done, which builds faith in what God can and will do in the future. As a result, in our telling of the testimony, we declare that we would like to see the Lord "do it again!"

I wish I had the space to share all of the incredible testimonies of salvations, physical healings, emotional healings, supernatural provision, freedom, restored marriages, etc., that Sozo Church has experienced over the past year. But that's for another book. All I can say is **Lord, do it again**!

So, what is your "KINGDOM OF HEAVEN is like" story?

THE ADVANCING KINGDOM

I've always been intrigued at how Jesus spent his final forty days on planet Earth. I mean the actual last days—after He had died on the cross, after the three days in the tomb, after He had raised from the dead and appeared to over five hundred people.

I mean, the final forty days that Jesus was with His disciples before He ascended to heaven.

In Acts 1:1-3, we learn that Jesus spent that entire forty days with His faithful followers, both teaching and doing things pertaining to the KINGDOM OF GOD.

In sharing our testimonies, we are declaring, "Lord, do it again!"

I'm sure He reminded them of some of His earlier messages. Like when He first began His ministry, quoting from Isaiah 61,

> *"The Spirit of the Lord is on me, because He has anointed me to preach good news to the poor. He has sent me to proclaim freedom to the prisoners and recovery of sight to the blind, to set the oppressed free, to proclaim the year of the Lord's favor"* (Luke 4:18-19).

JESUS' GOOD NEWS of the KINGDOM is that the manifestation of God's ruling presence has come to planet Earth to offer forgiveness, freedom, grace, power, and purpose. This message was so important that He had to make sure that they "got it" so they could live it out and pass it on after He was gone.

Jesus had declared prior to his death,

> *"This gospel of the kingdom will be preached in the whole world as a testimony to all the nations, and then the end will come"* (Matthew 24:14 NASB).

Not surprisingly, each of Jesus' disciples and all the early writers of the New Testament taught about the KINGDOM OF GOD. The next time you read the letters of Peter, John, or James, or Luke's incredible story of the early church in Acts, look for their "KINGDOM OF GOD is like" stories. Crawl into the skin of these characters. You'll soon find that what you once may have perceived as dry doctrine or dead history of the past has now been transformed into the incredible adventure of fellow sojourners on mission with God. The next time you read Paul's letters, picture Paul himself retelling his "KINGDOM OF GOD is like" stories. Try to imagine Paul's entire life as a revolutionary parable of the KINGDOM.

Reading through the first few chapters of Acts, one gets a sense of what Jesus expected normal KINGDOM OF GOD living to be like. In Acts 1 Jesus says,

> ". . . wait (in Jerusalem) for the gift my Father promised . . . you will be baptized with the Holy Spirit . . . you will receive power when the Holy Spirit comes on you; and you will be my witnesses in Jerusalem, and in all Judea and Samaria, and to the ends of the earth" (Acts 1:4-5, 8–parenthesis is mine).

Then immediately after these words of what normal Christ-life will be like, Jesus is taken up before their very eyes, and a cloud hides Him from their sight (Acts 1:9). What I want you to notice is four manifestations that occur continuously in the newborn church (Acts 2) that are a natural part of the KINGDOM OF GOD and normal Christianity.

UNIFIED PRAYER

The first thing the disciples did after gathering in an Upper Room to wait for the promised coming of the Holy Spirit was to **pray**. This was uncharted territory for them. No one had ever been baptized in the Holy Spirit before, with the promise of being indwelled permanently.

> *"They all joined together constantly in prayer, along with the women and Mary the mother of Jesus, and with his brothers . . . a group numbering about a hundred and twenty"* (Acts 1:14-15).

Jesus' crucifixion, resurrection, and enthronement is His finished work. Unified prayer is our partnering work with the purposes of the KINGDOM! (See Acts 3:1, 6-10 and Acts 4:23-31 for further examples of the dependence on and influence of prayer in the early church.)

SUPERNATURAL DEMONSTRATION

After ten days of constant prayer while waiting for the coming of the Holy Spirit in life-transforming power, the prayer of those 120 faithful was finally realized.

> *"When the day of Pentecost came, they were all together in one place (in Jerusalem, in constant prayer). Suddenly, a sound like the blowing of a violent wind came from heaven and filled the whole house . . . They saw what seemed to be tongues of fire that separated and came to rest on each of them. All were filled with the Holy Spirit and began to speak in other tongues as the Spirit enabled them"* (Acts 2:1-4— parenthesis is mine).

Even metaphorically, when your head catches on fire and your tongue is sanctified with a new language, that qualifies as a supernatural demonstration. (See Acts 3:6-10 and Acts 4:13-20 for further examples of the supernatural demonstration of normal Christianity.)

BOLD PROCLAMATION

The coming of the Holy Spirit in power has corresponding purpose and responsibility. But, as you might guess, the onlooking crowd had various opinions:

> *When they heard this sound, a crowd came together in bewilderment, because each one heard their own language being spoken. Utterly amazed, they asked: Aren't all these who are speaking Galileans? (They don't speak my language) . . . Amazed and perplexed, they asked one another, "What does this mean?" Some, however, made fun of them and said, "They have had too much wine"* (Acts 2:6-7, 12-13–parenthesis is mine).

This was the perfect set up for Peter's bold proclamation of the GOSPEL message.

> *"These people are not drunk, as you suppose. It's only nine in the morning! No, this (what you have experienced today) is what was spoken by the prophet Joel: 'In the last days, God says, I will pour out my Spirit on all people. Your sons and daughters will prophesy, your young men will see visions, your old men will dream dreams . . . everyone who calls upon the name of the Lord will be saved"* (Acts 2:15-21—parenthesis is mine).

CITY TRANSFORMATION
📖 Acts 1:8

The result of Peter's Pentecost message is found in Acts 2:37-41.

When the people heard this message, they were cut to the heart and said to Peter and the other apostles, "Brothers what shall we do?" Peter replied, "Repent and be baptized, every one of you, in the name of Jesus Christ for the forgiveness of your sins. And you will receive the gift of the Holy Spirit." Those who accepted his message were baptized, and about three thousand were added to their number that day.

A.D. 100
25,000 Jesus followers

A.D. 310
20 million Jesus followers

TODAY
Over 2.3 billion followers of Jesus—one out of every three people on our planet claim to be a follower of Jesus.[4]

In time, this group of spiritual revolutionaries would be known as those who turned the world upside-down with the message of Jesus and the KINGDOM OF GOD (Acts 17:6). (See Acts 4:1-20 and Acts 5:12-42 for further examples of city transformation through the power of the GOSPEL OF THE KINGDOM and NEW COVENANT.)

Tragically, today what we call "revival" is actually what Jesus expected the new normal of Christ-following to look like. We are NEW COVENANT ambassadors of the KINGDOM OF GOD, the manifestation of God's ruling presence.

So, is the KINGDOM advancing today?

Contrary to what doomsday prophets and pessimistic defeatists say, the church is not being defeated. She is not at the mercy of the devil or fallen society. The truth is, the KINGDOM OF HEAVEN is expanding, advancing, and growing like never before in the history of mankind. We simply need a better lens to see what our Father is up to.

Be reminded that Jesus said the KINGDOM OF HEAVEN is like a mustard seed that starts out extremely small (almost invisible); it becomes a bush, then a tree, and then the largest tree of the garden.

- The KINGDOM OF HEAVEN is like yeast that starts out as a small ratio but works its way into the dough until it has great effect.

- The KINGDOM OF HEAVEN is like hidden treasure and a pearl of great price: worth selling everything in order to obtain it.

- The KINGDOM OF HEAVEN is like a net with all kinds of fish! **All** are welcome into the KINGDOM OF GOD.

As believers of Christ:

We have been *"made competent as ministers of the new covenant —not of the letter, but of the Spirit; for the letter kills, but the Spirit gives life"* (2 Corinthians 3:6).

"(We) spread the aroma of the knowledge of Jesus everywhere (we go)" (2 Corinthians 2:14—parenthesis is mine).

We live from the promise: *"If anyone is in Christ, the new creation has come: The old has gone, the new is here!"* (2 Corinthians 5:17).

Like the disciples of old, we must rediscover the revolution of God. We must rediscover the adventure of our KINGDOM mission and daily ask ourselves the question: Where did I encounter Jesus today?

May normal, everyday encounters become KINGDOM adventures. We only have one life to live; let's choose to live a great story. Our stories matter! Our collective stories are creating a Jesus Movement that is radically affecting this generation and advancing the KINGDOM OF GOD on earth.

GRACE REFLECTIONS

1. Have you joined the KINGDOM movement?

   - Jesus said, "The time has come, the KINGDOM OF GOD has come near. Repent and believe the GOOD NEWS" (Mark 1:15).

   - Joining the KINGDOM OF GOD requires **humility**. It requires admitting that Jesus is King (Lord) and I am not. Humility releases **grace** for KINGDOM living.

   - "God opposes the proud but gives grace to the humble" (1 Peter 5:5).

   - Grace is more than unearned favor: grace is God's empowering Presence that enables you to be who Father created you to be and to do what He has called you to do.

2. Will you humble yourself, change your way of thinking to align with your heavenly Father's, and receive Jesus the King, by grace through faith?

3. Make this your prayer:

> "Father, I am so grateful for Your love that was demonstrated in Your sending Jesus to die for me, that my sins may be forgiven and that I may be reconciled to You.
>
> I now receive your free gift of salvation by faith.
>
> I trust my life to you, Father.
>
> I trust Jesus as the risen Savior and King of my life.
>
> I embrace Your love, receive the power and life of the Holy Spirit, and thank You that I am a new creation—the old has passed away and the new me has received new life today!"

May normal, everyday encounters become KINGDOM adventures. We only have one life to live—let's choose to live a great story!

If you received your salvation (forgiveness of sin) and the life that Jesus secured for you through His death and resurrection —Welcome to the KINGDOM family!

4. Now that you are in the KINGDOM family, earnestly make Matthew 6:33 your daily obsession. It was Jesus' obsession!

5. The only thing Jesus ever exhorted anyone to seek first is the KINGDOM OF GOD and His righteousness:
   "But seek first the kingdom of God and His righteousness, and all these things shall be added to you" (Matthew 6:33).

   "For the kingdom of God is not a matter of eating and drinking, but of righteousness, peace and joy in the Holy Spirit, because anyone who serves Christ in this way is pleasing to God and receives human approval" (Romans 14:17-18).

Enjoy your new glasses. You'll never view Scripture the same now that you see through the better lens of the NEW COVENANT and the KINGDOM OF GOD.

APPENDIX

Why Use the Language of Better Covenant Instead of New Covenant?

Perhaps, as you have been reading this book, you've wondered why I (the author) have chosen to use the language of BETTER COVENANT instead of NEW COVENANT in the subtitle and throughout the book. The truth is I really like the language of NEW COVENANT, because it is simple and thoroughly biblical. Unfortunately, the language of NEW COVENANT theology and BETTER COVENANT theology has different meanings for theologians in our day. I chose to remove confusion for my academic friends. That's the short answer. But if you're like me, you are probably asking, "So what's the difference between covenant theology, NEW COVENANT theology and BETTER COVENANT theology?"

We have all been handed a theological lens with which to read and interpret Scripture. Many of us unknowingly received a specific way of interpreting the Bible. For example, I was given a dispensational lens. Though no one ever told me that dispensationalism was the theological lens of our church, nevertheless, it was the filter through which I learned to read the Bible.

Growing up in the early 1970s, I witnessed dispensational theology as the rage of Western evangelicalism. My dad had a *Ryrie Study Bible,* and my mom had a copy of Hal Lindsey's *Late Great Planet Earth* on the nightstand by her bed. Both Charles Ryrie and Hal Lindsey were graduates of Dallas Theological Seminary, known for popularizing the theological system called "dispensationalism."

Here's a little background on the rise of dispensationalism. It was created and systematized by John Nelson Darby in the 1830s. However, dispensationalism did not gain traction until the early 1900s when Darby's notes were placed inside of C.I. Scofield's newly created "study Bible." Today, one can hardly imagine how influential this first-of-its-kind study Bible was. Never before had individuals been offered the opportunity to have a commentary inside of their Bible. Formerly, the sheer expense of purchasing a library of commentaries to use while studying the Bible had prohibited in-depth theological study by the vast majority of Christians. The *Scofield Study Bible* made theological study possible for all. The only issue was that the masses of Western evangelical Christianity were being indoctrinated with the singular lens of dispensationalism.

Dispensational theology began to spread in earnest when it was embraced by Chicago evangelist D.L. Moody and began to be taught to ministerial students at Moody Bible Institute in the early 1900s. With the founding of Dallas Theological Seminary in 1924 and its full acceptance of dispensationalism, an entire generation of evangelical ministers and their congregations became immersed in the dispensational approach to studying the Bible.

By the 1970s when I was coming of age to study the Bible, dispensationalism was already well entrenched as the theological lens of many Western evangelical circles.

DISPENSATIONALISM

Dispensationalism is so named because it is built on the foundation of dividing the Bible into seven major dispensations or historical time periods. Though not technically a type of covenant theology, dispensational ages do overlap the covenants God established in Scripture:

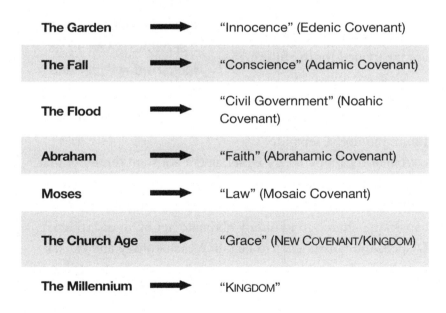

The Garden	➡	"Innocence" (Edenic Covenant)
The Fall	➡	"Conscience" (Adamic Covenant)
The Flood	➡	"Civil Government" (Noahic Covenant)
Abraham	➡	"Faith" (Abrahamic Covenant)
Moses	➡	"Law" (Mosaic Covenant)
The Church Age	➡	"Grace" (NEW COVENANT/KINGDOM)
The Millennium	➡	"KINGDOM"

Notice that dispensationalism relegates the KINGDOM OF GOD to the future. Thus, the eschatology of dispensationalism is known as Futurism. It must also be noted that most dispensationalists believe the Law of Moses will return in the Millennium.

Dr. Jonathan Welton writes, "God creates a plan, humankind begins walking it out, but it eventually fails, and as a result God must start over with a new dispensation. In this way, dispensationalism is in part a fatalistic system because it paints a filter over Scripture that always ends in utter failure."[34]

With regard to the NEW COVENANT, dispensational theology teaches that the NEW COVENANT is strictly for Israel and possibly, in a minor sense, for Christ-followers. It mixes eschatology and covenant to create a system where most biblical promises are postponed for the future.

Most are aware of dispensationalism because of its eschatology that espouses a future rapture, a separate covenant for modern-day Israel, and a constant reminder that we are living in the last days.

Most are aware of dispensationalism because of its eschatology that espouses a future rapture, a separate covenant for modern-day Israel, and a constant reminder that we are living in the last days. As Welton alluded to previously, futuristic dispensationalism creates an escapist mentality that causes the church to willingly abdicate her cultural influence. Dispensationalism leads to negative eschatology and causes people to struggle with the concept of advancing the KINGDOM.

Because each of its dispensations are separate, there is no progressive revelation leading to Jesus and His church. Therefore, the church is seen as merely a parenthesis (or mystery) in God's greater plan with Israel.

I will not take the time necessary to unpack in detail each of the four primary covenant theologies but will provide a short list of scholars from each position so you can study for yourself. Some of the prominent dispensational scholars include Charles C. Ryrie, C. I. Scofield, John Walvoord, J. Dwight Pentecost, and of course, John Darby.

COVENANT THEOLOGY

The next stop on my theological journey was covenant theology. While dispensationalism makes a clear distinction between Israel and the church, covenant theology unites God's people of all time into one church, teaching that the church fulfills the promises of the Old Testament, and thus becoming New Israel (Galatians 3:24-29; Ephesians 2:14-22). This is a major upgrade in unity. But, covenant theology still does not go far enough.

> "Covenant theology sees history as one continuous line, believing that God has interacted with humankind in the same manner all throughout history, and that each covenant is built on top of the previous. Thus, a covenant theologian would say the New Covenant revealed in the New Testament is a renewal of the Old Covenant. It is the same covenant, only updated and upgraded.[35]

> "Covenant theology divides the Old Testament Law into three parts: ceremonial laws, civil laws, and moral laws. The problem is that the Bible does not actually do this. The confusion of covenant theology is always, 'What do we keep, and what did Jesus remove?'"[36]

After listing dozens of OLD COVENANT laws, such as, *"Your male and female slaves are to come from the nations around you . . ."* (Leviticus 25:44), Dr. Stan Newton asks a difficult question: "Are all these laws of Moses really from the heart of

God? Are any in conflict with our understanding of the character of God, His very nature? Without questioning the inspiration of Scripture, could it be these Laws for the ancient Hebrews came because of necessity? They were to be a separate nation and therefore needed special protection. It was never God's plan for His people to live under such restrictions. There is a need for biblical scholars to address difficult questions most are afraid to ask. At this stage all I can say is, thank God for the NEW COVENANT!"[37]

Should Jesus followers keep the Law of Moses? Is bacon okay? How about tattoos? Who gets to make the call? Well, I think Hebrews 8 makes the call:

> [7]*For if there had been nothing wrong with that first covenant, no place would have been sought for another. [8]But God found fault with the people and said: "The days are coming, declares the Lord, when I will make a new covenant with the people of Israel and with the people of Judah. [9]It will not be like the covenant I made with their ancestors when I took them by the hand to lead them out of Egypt, because they did not remain faithful to my covenant, and I turned away from them, declares the Lord. [10]This is the covenant I will establish with the people of Israel after that time, declares the Lord. I will put my laws in their mind and write them on their hearts. I will be their God, and they will be my people."*

In Hebrews 8:7-10, we clearly see that the NEW COVENANT is not an upgrade or a renewal of the old Mosaic covenant. The NEW COVENANT is something completely new and different!

Covenant theology has been the dominant view of most reformed theologians. Start with John Calvin and follow the long trail.

NEW COVENANT THEOLOGY

The third stop on my journey to BETTER COVENANT theology was NEW COVENANT theology. This is where semantics in the academic world can become confusing. Initially, I assumed that NEW COVENANT theology and BETTER COVENANT theology are synonymous. Not so!

Theopedia, a growing online evangelical encyclopedia of biblical Christianity, states:

"New Covenant Theology refers to a theological view of redemptive history primarily found in Baptist circles and contrasted with Covenant theology and dispensationalism. It has been assumed that one has only two primary options in understanding the structure of the Bible in evangelical Christianity—Covenant Theology (coming out of the Reformation in the 1500s) or dispensationalism (from Darby in the 1830s). However, proponents see New Covenant Theology (NCT) as middle ground with a biblical basis of understanding."[38]

Fred Zaspel, a NEW COVENANT Theology author, writes:

"New Covenant Theology is less a settled theology than a movement still in the shaping by men who agree that the question has not yet been finally answered by either of the major competing schools of interpretation—Dispensational Theology and Covenant Theology. There are still disagreements among us on several details, such as the questions of the future of ethnic/national Israel and the Millennium."[39]

In *The Death of the Messiah and the Birth of the New Covenant*, Michael J Gorman writes,

"With respect to the concern about supersessionism or anti-Judaism, the first thing to be said is that the idea of a new covenant does not make sense except, first of all, as a category of Jewish identity and theology. The appropriate perspective of the Christian faith, therefore, is that the new covenant in which it claims to participate is not a replacement covenant but a renewed covenant . . . In a way not unlike the kingdom of God, the new covenant is both now and not yet."[40]

Gorman's rhetoric of the NEW COVENANT being a "renewed" covenant and not a *new* covenant is concerning language for an avowed NEW COVENANT theologian. I understand that the very word "replacement" or "new" sends up red flags for many Zionists, but if the NEW COVENANT is not truly *new*, what do we do with Hebrews 8-10?

I understand that being branded a "replacement theologian" is a curse few want to incur, but I think it's vital that we not sidestep the fact that the NEW COVENANT is nothing like the OLD COVENANT; it is not a renewal.

The days are coming, declares the Lord, when I will make a new covenant . . . It will not be like the covenant I made with their ancestors (Hebrews 8:8-9).

Dr. Stan Newton's assessment of NEW COVENANT theology resonates with me. He says,

"As we progress toward a new way of understanding covenant, we can use 'some' of the New Covenant arguments. The reason NCT is a non-starter in my (Newton's) mind is based on three areas of difficulty:

• "The NCT position is not clear about what part of the Mosaic Law enters the New Covenant. Until it is, I (Newton) cannot support it."

- "That early NCT practitioners appear to have a lack of appreciation for the Holy Spirit in the New Covenant is problematic. Their views are not clearly stated, thus leaving room for the influence of cessationism. While this may only slightly change the basic system of theology, it will have a HUGE impact on the application of the theology."

- "NCT's insistence that covenant and eschatology must be viewed separately is a game-changer. This may seem small, since I (Newton) agree on many points, but it is paramount as to how one sees the ongoing work of the Kingdom in the New Covenant."[41]

For further study of NEW COVENANT theology, you can start with the authors I have listed in this section: Fred G. Zaspel and Michael J. Gorman.

Few, if any, are more thoroughly researched, insightful, and succinct in their writings about BETTER COVENANT Theology than Dr. Jonathan Welton. It was Welton who officially coined the term BETTER COVENANT Theology (BCT) in April 2013. Since then, it has been rapidly gaining acceptance as an alternative to Dispensational Theology, Covenant Theology, and NEW COVENANT Theology in both academic and church communities.

There will certainly need to be much rigorous discussion, alteration, and practical time-tested living out of this theology to prove BCT's true value and worth. But, though early in its development, I believe BCT offers a way forward for a better theology. One that truly is the GOOD NEWS of the KINGDOM OF GOD.

BETTER COVENANT THEOLOGY

The current position in my unfolding theological journey is called Better Covenant Theology. After exploring three possible lenses for seeing God's covenant purposes with mankind, it became apparent that another option was needed: one that would allow us to accurately view the heart, mind, and activity of God—today! We need a theology that truly expresses the superior covenant and better promises we are now and forevermore engaged in with God (our Father, Savior, Spirit). We need a BETTER COVENANT theology!

As Stan Newton has written:

> "We need a covenant that clearly divides history; a time before Christ, and time on the right side of the Cross. We need a covenant that makes Jesus Christ the center of history and theology. We need a better view that stays true to the message of new creation and embraces a present and advancing Kingdom of God. We need a view that gives the Spirit His proper role as administrator of this new covenant.
>
> "We need a better covenant—one that is guaranteed by Jesus (Hebrews 7:22)."[42]

TEN PILLARS OF BETTER COVENANT THEOLOGY[43]

Jesus' birth fulfilled the Abrahamic Covenant.
↳ *Matthew 1:1; Galatians 3:16; Acts 3:24-26*

Jesus' death created a NEW COVENANT.
↳ *Hebrews 9:14-15*

3 The NEW COVENANT is between the Father, (as God), and the Son (as High Priest in the order of Melchizedek).
↳ *Hebrews 5:5*

4 Jesus' ascension and enthronement in heaven fulfilled the Davidic KINGDOM promises.
↳ *Matthew 1:1; Acts 2:29-36*

5 The destruction of Jerusalem in AD 70 removed the OLD COVENANT permanently and fulfilled Hebrews 8:13.
↳ *Hebrews 8:13; also Hebrews 7:12, 10:9*

6 Between the cross and AD 70 existed a forty-year covenant transition for the early church.
↳ *Acts 6:13-15, 21:21; Galatians 4:28-30*

7 During the transition period, the OLD COVENANT and the NEW COVENANT co-existed.
↳ *1 Corinthians 2:6; Hebrews 8:13, 9:8-10; 1 John 2:8*

8 The end of the age and the last days were first-century references to the last days of the OLD COVENANT and the end of the OLD COVENANT age.

9 No application of the Mosaic OLD COVENANT remains; the feasts, Sabbaths, civil laws, ceremonial laws, and moral laws are done away with.
↳ *Colossians 2:16-17; Ephesians 2:15; Galatians 4:10-11, 5:6; Hebrews 9:9-10*

10 The law of the NEW COVENANT is: "Love one another as I have loved you."
↳ *John 13:34, 15:12,17; 1 Cor. 9:19-22; Romans 8:2; 1 John 3:23; 2 John 1:6*

*The days are coming, declares the Lord, when I will make a new covenant . . . It will not be like the covenant I made with their ancestors . . . (*Hebrews 8:8-9).

By calling this covenant "new," He has made the first one obsolete; and what is obsolete and outdated will soon disappear (Hebrews 8:13).

Therefore, brothers and sisters, since we have confidence to enter the Most Holy Place by the blood of Jesus, by a new and living way opened for us through the curtain, that is his body . . . let us draw near to God with a sincere heart and with full assurance that faith brings, having our hearts sprinkled to cleanse us from a guilty conscience and having our bodies washed with pure water (Hebrews 10:19-22).

For more information about BETTER COVENANT theology, I highly recommend the works of Stan Newton and Jonathan Welton.

NOTES

Introduction

    1. Simon Sinek, *Find Your Why,* (HESMotivation, September 27, 2017).
    2. Ibid.

Chapter 1

    3. C. Baxter Kruger, *Across All Worlds* (Regent College Publishing, Vancouver, British Columbia, 2007), 7-8.
    4. John MacMurray, *A Spiritual Evolution* (Open Table Press, 2018), 16-17.
    5. Sozo Church Core Beliefs, www.sozosmtx.com

Chapter 2

    6. Richard Dawkins, *The God Delusion* (New York: Bantam, 2006), 51.
    7. Sam Harris, *Letter to a Christian Nation* (New York: Bantam, 2007), 4.
    8. Brian Zahnd, GoodCast, Episode 3 "Sinners in the Hand of a Loving God." (August 25, 2017).
    9. Andy Stanley, "First Things First," *Irresistible* (Zondervan, 2018), 294.
    10. Brian Zahnd, *Sinners in the Hands of a Loving God,* (WaterBrook, Imprint of Crown Publishing Group, 2017), 31.
    11. Ibid, 63, 50.
    12. Conversation with Wayne Jacobsen in Boerne, Texas, 2013. For more, see www.lifestream.org/TheJesusLens.
    13. Rob Bell, Episode 8: The Enduring Relevance, Astonishing Power, and Unexpected Brilliance of the Bible, The Rob Cast, robbell.podbean.com, March 8, 2015. [Note: *While I do not agree with some of Bell's theology, his thoughts on progressive revelation in this podcast are very helpful.*]
    14. Zahnd, *Sinners in the Hands of a Loving God, 15.*
    15. Bell, Episode 8, The Rob Cast.

Chapter 3

    16. Bill Johnson, *God Is Good* (Destiny Image Publications, 2016), 36.

Chapter 4

    17. C. Baxter Kruger, *Parable of the Dancing God,* (Perichoresis Press, 1994), note on inside back cover.
    18. Jack R. Taylor, *Cosmic Initiative* (Whitaker House, 2017), 32-33.
    19. Kruger, *Across All Worlds*, 7.
    20. Bill Johnson, *God Is Good* (Destiny Image Publishers, 2016), 49-50.
    21. Ibid, 50.

22. Scott Hahn, *Kinship by Covenant* (New Haven, CT: Yale University Press, 2009), 29-30. On page 30, Hahn includes a chart listing several authors who confirm details of the three types of covenants.
23. Kevin Conner & Ken Malmin, *The Covenants* (Bible Temple Publishing, 1983), 4.
24. Jonathan Welton, *New Covenant Revolution,* (Welton Academy, 2016), 2.

Chapter 5

25. Roger Fields and Jeff Fields, *Breaking the Hex* (Broken Egg Press, 2017), p.66, 68.
26. Dan McCollam, Living on the Right Side of the Cross—CD series disc 1 (Sounds of the Nations, Vacaville, CA).
27. Ibid.
28. Ted Dekker with Bill Vanderbush, *The Forgotten Way Study Guide,* (Outlaw Studios, 2015), 5.
29. McCollam, Living on the Right Side of the Cross—CD series disc 1 (Sounds of the Nations, Vacaville, CA). Grace reflections, prayer, and activation are taken from this talk.

Chapter 6

30. Brian McClaren, *The Secret Message of Jesus* (W Publishing Group, a Division of Thomas Nelson, Inc.,2006), 13.
31. Ibid.16.
32. Ray Vander Laan, recording of a lecture series he did for a Focus on the Family training, 2007.
33. Alan Hirsch, *The Forgotten Ways*, (Brazos Press, 2006), 18. From R. Stark, *The Rise of Christianity,* (San Francisco: Harper Collins, 1996), 6-13.

Appendix

34. Jonathan Welton, *Understanding the Whole Bible*, (Jon Welton Ministries, 2014), 96, 98.
35. Welton, *Understanding the Whole Bible*, 99.
36. Ibid, 99-100.
37. Stan Newton, *Glorious Covenant,* (Vision Publishing), 44.
38. Ibid, 55.
39. Fred G. Zaspel, *A Brief Explanation of the New Covenant Theology,* www.biblical studies.
40. Michael J. Gorman, *The Death of the Messiah and the Birth of the New Covenant*, (Cascade Books, 2014), 23.
41. Newton, *Glorious Covenant*, 60.
42. Ibid, 63.
43. Jonathan Welton, *New Covenant Revolution* (Welton Academy, 2016), 9-10.

Made in the USA
Coppell, TX
14 February 2020

15825083R10098